Winning
POKER
SYSTEMS

Winning POKER SYSTEMS

♦ ♠ ♣ ♥

by *Norman Zadeh*

PRENTICE-HALL, INC., *Englewood Cliffs, N.J.*

Prentice-Hall International, Inc., London
Prentice-Hall of Australia, Pty. Ltd., Sydney
Prentice-Hall of Canada, Ltd., Toronto
Prentice-Hall of India Private Ltd., New Delhi
Prentice-Hall of Japan, Inc., Tokyo

10 9 8 7 6 5 4 3 2

Library of Congress Cataloging in Publication Data
Zadeh, Norman
   Winning poker systems.
   1. Poker.   I. Title.
GV1251.Z32   795.4'12   74-5234
ISBN 0-13-961292-0

ACKNOWLEDGMENTS

I would like to thank a close friend in California for his assistance with the manuscript. Thanks are also due to Bram Cavin of Prentice-Hall, Oscar Collier, and the team at Prentice-Hall that designed and edited this book.

CONTENTS

INTRODUCTION

Poker, America's favorite card game, is played legally and illegally all over the world for stakes ranging from pennies to thousands of dollars. In 1960 it was estimated that 47 million Americans wagered $75 billion at some form of poker. Many people feel that poker is a game of luck. That is not so. Just as with chess or bridge, there are right plays and wrong plays in poker, and the player who makes the right play more often will win. If he always makes the right play, he will win spectacularly.

By using probability theory with the aid of an electronic computer, the author has computed what the right or best plays are in most of the situations that occur in Straight Draw Poker, Jacks or Better Draw Poker, and Lowball. Stud Poker and High-Low were also analyzed, and valuable new information about these games is presented.

The systems developed for Draw Poker and Lowball have been acknowledged by several of the country's best players to be more powerful than anything which they have used. These players are currently using the systems professionally with great success.

For those who find it difficult to believe that a winning system can be constructed for a complex game like poker, the Appendix presents examples of how some of the strategies were computed. Approximately six months were required to compute and check all the strategies.

It is fortunate and perhaps surprising that no card-playing experience is needed to use the basic system. This system requires only that one count the money in the pot and determine his "position" relative to the dealer. As the reader becomes familiar with his opponents, he can then switch to a system that takes their betting habits into account and is extremely powerful. Either system will beat any-one except cheats and possibly a few great players. To avoid being cheated, the reader should play in a game with people he knows, or in a legal club game that has a good reputation.

In the ensuing pages I begin with an introductory section for the benefit of beginning players. The rules of Draw Poker and Stud Poker are explained, and several sample deals are analyzed. We then proceed step by step to cover the important topics of limits, pot odds, and position.

In Chapters 3, 4, 5, and 6, the systems for Draw Poker and Lowball are presented. These systems show the reader what hands to bet with, raise with, and bluff with. They are easy to use and understand.

Along with the systems, a number of odds tables are in-cluded, the majority of which are new. Probably the most useful are those that give the chances of various hands' winning in actual playing situations. For example, in Seven-Card Stud, a player starting with $\underline{KK}2$ has a 65.7% chance of beating a player starting with $\underline{88}3$. Tables of this kind are given for Draw Poker; Lowball; Five-, Six-, and Seven-Card Stud; and Five-, Six-, and Seven-Card Stud for low.

Advanced players should be particularly interested in the treatment given here of Stud and High-Low. Calling rules are presented for these games that allow a player to make very accurate calling decisions. The topic of reading hands is discussed in considerable detail. Each stud game is analyzed for both high and low limits. High-Low Draw is covered in detail, along with High-Low Seven-Card Stud.

In Chapter 9, a system of general rules is presented that may be used to analyze a wide variety of situations. In the Appendix, a demonstration is given as to how various strategies were actually computed.

In short, this book is for both beginners and experts. Anyone who reads *Winning Poker Systems* should gain a substantial edge which will reward him handsomely at the table. Those of you who take full advantage of the book can expect to win in almost any game in the country.

Winning
POKER
SYSTEMS

1

BASICS

HOW POKER IS PLAYED

There are many different kinds of poker, but they are all played in approximately the same way. Each player is dealt a number of cards (usually five) to form a hand. Players wager (bet) various amounts of money based on the value of their hands. After the betting has ended, the hands are shown, and the best hand wins what has been bet (the pot).

Anyone can play poker once he learns two things: the ranks (values) of the poker hands, and the rules of betting. Let's look at the hands first.

POKER HANDS

Poker hands consist of five cards. They are ranked as shown below, best hands first. Readers interested in playing immediately should concentrate on learning the last three categories (7, 8, and 9), which contain most of the hands encountered in actual play.

1. Straight Flush: a sequence of five cards of the same suit. Examples: ◆A◆K◆Q◆J◆10, ♥9♥8♥7♥6♥5, ♣6♣5♣4♣3♣2.
2. Four of a Kind. Examples: KKKK4, 8888A, 44447.
3. Full House: three cards of one rank and two of another. Examples: 88866, 444JJ, 222AA.
4. Flush: five cards of the same suit, but not in sequence.

Examples: ◆A◆6◆5◆3◆2, ♥K♥10♥4♥3♥2, ♠Q♠8♠5 ♠3♠2.

5. Straight: five cards in sequence, but not of the same suit. Examples: KQJ109, 98765, 76543.
6. Three of a Kind (Trips). Examples: KKK42, 888A10, 77743.
7. Two Pairs. Examples: KK442, QQ88A, 6655K.
8. One Pair. Examples: AA432, QQK84, 88J42.
9. No Pair: five odd cards. Examples: AK642, Q10852, 85432.

The ranking of individual cards in descending order is A, K, Q, J, 10, 9, 8, 7, 6, 5, 4, 3, 2. Hands in any particular category are also ranked. This ranking is done by comparing the ranks of certain "key" cards in the hands. For example, since an eight is higher than a four, 88882 beats 4444A, 88822 beats 444KK, 888KQ beats 44496, 8822K beats 4433A, and 88K42 beats 44QJ10. Because a queen is higher than a jack, AAQQ2 beats AAJJ10, AAQ32 beats AAJ109, Q5432 of spades beats J10842 of spades, Q7432 beats J10964, and AKQ32 beats AKJ109, etc.

There is no distinction between suits. In other words, AKQJ8 of hearts ties AKQJ8 of spades.

A good exercise at this point is to deal a pack of cards into ten groups of five and arrange the groups in order of value as poker hands. Beginning readers should do this three or four times, as it will make the rest of the chapter much easier to read. If you don't have a deck, you can practice with the hands listed below.

(a) ♣4♥4♠K◆Q♠10
(b) ♠Q♥Q♥A♥9♠6
(c) ◆A◆K♠8♥5◆3
(d) ◆10◆9◆5♥3◆2
(e) ♣A♠J♣9♥6♣5
(f) ♠4◆4♠2♣2♥10
(g) ◆J♣J♠A♣K♠9
(h) ♥K♣Q♣8♠7♠5
(i) ♣7♥7♠3♣3♥2
(j) ♣6◆6♥J♣10◆7

Answer: i, f, b, g, j, a, c, e, h, d.

A SAMPLE DEAL OF DRAW POKER

Once you have learned the poker hands, the next and last step is to learn the rules of betting for the two basic forms of poker: Draw and Stud. Probably the easiest way to do this is to examine a sample deal of each. Let's look at Draw first.

The players in a typical game are seated as shown in Figure 1.1. In general, there need not be eight players. Play starts when each player *antes* by putting, say, 25¢ in the center of the table. This makes an initial *pot* of $2. I call this initial pot the *total ante*. Richard has been elected to deal, and deals five cards facedown to each player. The cards dealt to each player are shown in Table 1.1. Each player picks up his cards and examines them. Then the first round of betting begins.

Pam, the player to the dealer's left, must speak first. She has two choices. She may either bet by putting some money into the pot, or she may *pass* (*check*). Since her hand is poor (it consists of five odd cards), she passes. The players act in a clockwise order, so it is now Arch's turn. He has the same options that Pam had.

FIGURE 1.1
The Players in a Typical Poker Game

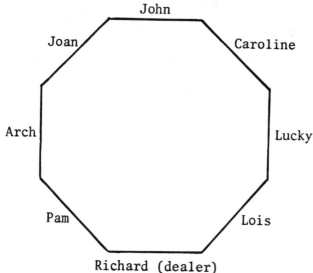

Arch has a fairly good hand (a pair of aces), so he *opens* the pot by betting, say, $1.

TABLE 1.1
The Cards Dealt to Each Player

Pam	♥A♠J♥10♠9♠7
Arch	♦A♣A♠K♣4♣2
Joan	♣J♦J♠Q♣8♦3
John	♠A♣K♣10♥7♠2
Caroline	♠8♠7♠4♠3♥2
Lucky	♦Q♥Q♦4♣4♥3
Lois	♣Q♦10♣9♥8♦5
Richard	♥J♥9♦7♦6♦2

(Players are listed in the order in which they speak.)

After the pot is opened, each player in turn has one of three choices: He may either *fold, call,* or *raise.* A player folds or drops by throwing in his cards. He calls by putting in enough money so that his total contribution equals that of the player who bet or raised just before him. He raises by putting in more than is required to call.

The mechanics behind calling and raising will become clearer as we proceed with the deal. Arch opened for $1, so Joan may either call by putting in $1, raise by putting in more than $1, or fold by throwing in her cards. Joan figures that Arch must have a better hand so she folds. John folds, and so does Caroline. Lucky is next to speak. He has a good hand (two pairs) so he puts in $2. This means that he raises Arch $1. If Lois wants to call, it will cost her $2. She folds, and so does Richard. Pam may call or raise at this point even though she passed initially. However, she folds. It is now up to Arch. If he folds, Lucky will win the pot and a new deal will be started. Arch figures Lucky for a better hand, but since there is quite a lot of money in the pot, Arch calls. This ends the first betting round.

The draw now takes place for all those who have stayed. Arch, the active player to the dealer's left, must draw first.

TABLE 1.2
Summary of the Betting Before the Draw

Pam	Pass	Fold
Arch	Bet $1	Call
Joan	Fold	
John	Fold	
Caroline	Fold	
Lucky	Raise $1	
Lois	Fold	
Richard	Fold	

He may exchange any number of cards in his hand for new ones from the unused portion of the deck. Since the king, four, and deuce aren't helping him (he would like to have a pair in place of these cards, or perhaps another ace), he throws away the king, four, and deuce and requests (*draws*) three new cards. These are dealt to him facedown. Lucky throws away his three and draws one card. The new cards that Arch receives are Q, J, and 10. Lucky receives a K.

Now the second betting round begins. The rules for betting are the same as before. Arch, who opened, must speak first. He can either pass (check) or bet. He suspects that Lucky has a better hand, so he checks. Lucky checks also. At this point there is a *showdown*. (If Arch bet and Lucky called, there would also be a showdown. However, if Arch bet and Lucky dropped, Arch would win the pot.) Both players expose (*show*) their cards. Lucky has two pairs, which is higher than Arch's single pair. Consequently, Lucky wins the pot. After Lucky takes the money from the pot, everyone antes a quarter and a new deal is started. Pam, the player to Richard's left, is the new dealer.

Summary of Betting Rules

1. On the first round, the player to the dealer's left is first to speak. He may either bet or pass. If he passes, the player to his left has the same options. If all pass, there is a redeal.

2. When a player opens, the remaining players in turn may either fold, call, or raise.
3. If a player makes a bet or raise that no one calls, he wins the pot.
4. A betting interval ends when two or more players have put in the same amount of money and the rest of the players have folded.
5. During the draw, the player to the dealer's left must discard first.
6. After the draw, the opener speaks first. If he has dropped, the first player to speak is the active player to the opener's left.

A SAMPLE DEAL OF STUD

The betting rules for Stud are quite similar to those for Draw, but there are minor differences. I will illustrate by presenting a sample deal of what is known as Five-Card Stud.

The players, dealer, and ante are the same as before. However, instead of dealing five cards facedown to each player, Richard deals one card facedown and one card faceup. The cards dealt to each player are shown below. Cards dealt facedown, called *hole cards,* are underlined.

Pam	47
Arch	107
Joan	QQ
John	KA
Caroline	32
Lucky	Q5
Lois	74
Richard (dealer)	33

In Stud, the player with the best exposed hand (*board*) must speak first. In this case it is John, who shows an ace. John may either check or bet. Since he has a pretty good hand for Stud, he bets $1. Caroline, who is to John's left, now has three choices: She may either fold, call, or raise. Caroline folds. Lucky is next to speak and also folds, as does Lois. Richard has a pair of threes, which is a good starting hand, so he calls. Pam and Arch fold. Joan has a very good hand but merely calls, not wanting to scare out the other players. This ends the first betting round. Each active player is now dealt one more card, faceup. Joan receives a four, giving her QQ4; John receives a jack, giving him K̲AJ; and Richard deals himself a deuce, giving him 3̲32. Again, John, the high board, must speak first. He bets $2, and the others call. This ends the second betting round. Another upcard is dealt to each player. Joan receives a four, John a jack, and Richard a five. The hands are now: Joan, QQ44; John, K̲AJJ; and Richard, 3̲325. John, who is high, bets $4. Richard folds since he is beaten by both players. Joan calls. She is still *slowplaying* the best hand. The fifth (and last) cards are dealt. Joan receives a five, giving her QQ445. John receives a 3, giving him K̲AJJ3. John checks, whereupon Joan bets $10. John realizes that Joan has him beat and that his only hope is to *bluff*. He raises $20. This play persuades Joan to drop. John takes the pot.

In summary, Stud is played like draw except that:

1. Each player is initially dealt two cards, one down and one up. A betting round follows. Then another upcard. Then another betting round, and so forth, until five cards are dealt to each active player.
2. The player with the best board must speak first.

SIX- AND SEVEN-CARD STUD

Six- and Seven-Card Stud are played just like Five-Card Stud except that each player gets more cards. To begin, each player is dealt two cards facedown and one card faceup. A typical playable starting hand might be Q4Q̲ or 7̲7J. After the initial hands are dealt, the first betting round follows. Then another upcard. Then another betting round. This continues in Six-Card Stud until four cards are dealt faceup. In the showdown, the player who can form the best hand of five cards wins. Seven-Card Stud is played in a similar fashion except that one more card is dealt at the end, facedown.

TOTAL ANTE

The object of the ante at the beginning of each deal is to give the players something to play for. The total amount anted by all the players is called the *total ante*. If each of eight players puts in 25¢, the total ante is $2. If each of eight players puts in 10¢, the total ante is 80¢. The total ante is extremely important because many of the winning strategies depend upon its size. For example, when the total ante is "large," players should open, call, and raise with weaker hands.

LIMITS

In the sample deals there was no limit on the amount that players could bet or raise. In practice, some kind of limit is always imposed. The following types of limit are the most common.

1. *Flat or fixed limit.* Players may bet or raise any amount up to say $2. Sometimes the limit is increased after the draw. For example, the limit before the draw might be $2, and after the draw, $4.
2. *Pot limit.* The limit for any bet or raise is the amount of money in the pot at the time the bet or raise is made. If the pot contains $3, the maximum a player can bet is $3. A player who raises may count as part of the pot that money required for him to call. In other words, if there is $2 in the pot and it costs $1 to call, the next player can call for $1, increasing the pot to $3, and then raise $3.

3. *Table stakes.* In table stakes, no restriction is made on the size of a bet or raise. However, players cannot bet more than they have on the table. Table stakes is quite similar to pot limit because the correct bet in table stakes is often the size of the pot.

Comparison of Flat Limit and Pot Limit

The strategies computed for Draw and Lowball are applicable to either pot limit or flat limit games *after the draw*. Before the draw they are meant for flat limit and they must be adjusted for pot limit. Such an adjustment is necessary because of the considerable difference between pot limit and flat limit. We may see this difference by looking at an example.

Suppose first that your game has a total ante of $1 and a flat limit of $1. If you open for $1, your opponent can raise $1 and can bet $1 after the draw.

Now suppose that your game has a pot limit. Your opponent can raise $3 before the draw, and if you call, he can bet $9 afterwards. Obviously, you have more to fear when you open in pot limit. Therefore, you need a slightly better hand to do so. I say "slightly" because you won't run into pot-size bets or raises very often. Opponents need very good hands to bet or raise the pot.

Bet the Limit

Players can generally make any size bet up to the limit, but their correct bet will usually be the limit or the pot, whichever is smaller. *When I say that someone should bet, I will always mean that he should bet the limit, unless I state otherwise.* Thus the term "bet" will always refer to a limit-size bet.

Some players have the habit of betting more when they have a better hand. This is like telegraphing a punch. If you always bet the limit or the pot (whichever is smaller),

you won't give yourself the chance to make this kind of
mistake.

POT ODDS

At any point in the game the pot will contain a certain
amount of money, and it will cost a certain amount to bet
or call.* The ratio of the amount in the pot to the amount
required to bet or call is known as the odds offered by the
pot, or *pot odds.* For example, if the pot contains $4 and the
bet is $2, then the ratio of the pot to the bet is 4 to 2, so the
odds offered by the pot are 2 to 1. Similarly, if the pot contained $3 and the bet were $1, then the odds offered by the
pot would be 3 to 1.

This ratio has a profound effect on winning strategies.
In particular, *as the odds offered by the pot grow, the requirements
for betting, calling, and raising should decrease.* To see this,
simply consider what happens when the total ante in a game
is increased. In this case the players stand to gain more by
opening, so they can afford to open with weaker hands.
Once everyone starts opening with weaker hands, players
can then call and raise with less. As a result, all the requirements are reduced.

Because the winning strategy for a particular situation
may change if the size of the pot is changed, the odds offered
by the pot must be specified whenever a winning strategy
is presented. Otherwise, the reader will have no idea just
when that strategy is supposed to win.**

I prefer to specify pot odds in terms of the number of
"bets" in the pot. If a player wishes to bet $2, and the pot
contains $6, then the pot equals three $2 "bets." The odds
it offers are therefore 3 to 1. A pot of $8 equals four $2
"bets," and therefore offers odds of 4 to 1. Rather than say

---

* Remember, it is assumed throughout the book that the amount required to bet
or call is the limit. Any adjustments in strategy that should be made when players
bet less than the limit will be discussed in Chapter 3.
** It's interesting to note that many poker books do not mention pot odds when
they give advice.

that the pot odds are 4 to 1 or 3 to 1, I simply say that the pot contains 4 bets or 3 bets.

PASS AND OUT GAMES

You may have noticed in the sample deal of Draw Poker that a player who passed could later come back in to call or raise. All poker games allow players to pass (check) after the draw, but practice varies as to whether players may pass (check) before the draw. If a player is not allowed to pass on the first round, then a pass on his part is interpreted as a fold. In other words, if he passes, he is out. Games that consider a player to be out once he passes are called "pass and out" games. Games that allow a player to pass and later get back in are called "pass and back in" games. Both types of game are important, but pass and out games will be discussed first.

Table 1.3 (taken from Chapter 3) presents a typical set

TABLE 1.3
Opening Requirements for a Pass and Out Game
with a Total Ante of Two Bets*

Player	Number of Active Opponents	Minimum Hand Required to Open**
Pam	7	QQ
Arch	6	JJ
Joan	5	1010
John	4	88
Caroline	3	66
Lucky	2	22
Lois	1	Anything
Richard	0	——

* Recall that each bet is assumed to equal the limit. This caption essentially says that Table 1.3 is applicable to any game that has a total ante equaling two limit-size bets. For example, Table 1.3 applies to a game that has a total ante of $20 and a limit of $10. It also applies to a game that has a total ante of 10¢ and a limit of 5¢.

** One should also open with a four flush, e.g., ♣K♣Q♣8♣2♥4. The reason for this will be given in Chapter 3.

of opening requirements for a pass and out game. Let's see if we can get a feel for why the requirements in the table appear as they do. Let's look at Pam first. Pam is in the worst position, because she has to speak first and has seven opponents who may raise if she opens. As a result, she needs a fairly strong hand (at least queens) to open. (An explanation of how this hand was computed is presented in Section 1 of the Appendix.) Given that Pam needs queens, we may now ask what Arch needs. When Arch gets a chance to open, Pam will have passed, so Arch will only have six opponents to worry about. Because he has less competition, he can open with a weaker hand (jacks). A similar argument now applies to Joan. When Joan gets a chance to open, Pam and Arch will both have passed, so Joan will only have five opponents to worry about. Because she has even less competition, she can open with tens. The requirements continue to drop because each player in turn has less competition. When it is Lois's turn, she can open with anything,* because she only has Richard to worry about. Richard has the best position of all. If everyone else passes, he simply wins the pot.

Pass and Back In Games

In a pass and back in game, a player does not necessarily have to open if he has a strong hand. He may prefer to pass instead, so as to be in a position to raise if someone else opens. Players who pass in this fashion are said to be *sandbagging.*

Most pass and back in draw games are played with a requirement that one must have at least jacks to open. Such games are called *Jackpots.* (Jackpots is another name for Jacks or Better Draw Poker.) There are situations in Jackpots in which sandbagging is the correct play, but these situations occur primarily when the total ante is small (less than or equal to the limit). When the total ante is two or more times the limit, it hurts too much when the hand gets passed out, and sandbagging should generally be avoided. Table 1.4 (taken from Chapter 3) gives the correct

---

* This may be verified by using an argument similar to that given in Section 1 of the Appendix.

opening requirements for Jackpots when the total ante equals 2 bets. We will need to refer to it in Chapter 2.

TABLE 1.4
Opening Requirements for a Jackpots
Game with a Total Ante of Two Bets

Player	Players Yet to Speak	Minimum Hand Required to Open
Pam	7	QQ
Arch	6	JJ
Joan	5	JJ
John	4	JJ
Caroline	3	JJ
Lucky	2	JJ
Lois	1	JJ
Richard	0	JJ

POSITION

The importance of position in poker is best illustrated by the following figure, which is based on Table 1.3. It shows how the opening requirements for a player in a pass and out game depend on his position at the table. Observe that Pam, sitting to the left of the dealer, needs queens to open, whereas Lois, sitting to the dealer's right, can open with anything.

Besides affecting opening requirements, position also affects calling and raising requirements. To see this, suppose that someone opens, everyone else drops, and it is up to Richard. His correct strategy is affected by the position of the opener. If Lois opened, Richard could call with anything (Lois's excellent position allows her to open with anything), and he would only need a pair of fives to raise. However, if Pam opened the pot, Richard would have to play much tighter. Pam would figure to have at least queens, and it would be wrong for Richard to call with less than kings. He would need at least two pairs to raise.

Notice that position has an effect quite similar to pot odds. A player in a good position can bet with weaker

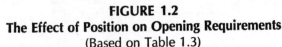

FIGURE 1.2
The Effect of Position on Opening Requirements
(Based on Table 1.3)

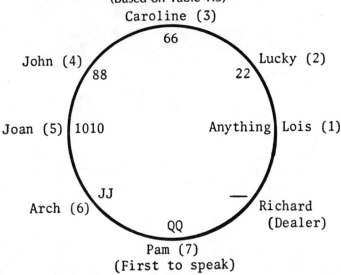

hands, and because of this, his opponents can call and raise with weaker hands. The result is that the betting, calling, and raising requirements are all reduced, as they would be if the pot were "large."

Because position is so important, it is essential that we have a convenient way to refer to the various positions at the table. Since the quality of a player's position is determined by the number of players who act after he does, I prefer to label the positions as indicated in Figure 1.3. In an eight-man game, the first player to speak is in position seven (seven players act after he does), and the dealer is in position zero (no one acts after he does). In a five-man game, the first player to speak is in position four (four players act after he does). This way of describing position may take a little getting used to, but I assure you that it's the right way to do it. Some people describe position by the order in which you speak, i.e., the player who speaks first is in first position, etc. The trouble with this approach is that being first to speak in a five-man game is quite different from being first to speak in an eight-man game.

FIGURE 1.3
A Convenient Way of Referring
to the Positions at a Table

POSITION BEFORE THE DRAW IN AN EIGHT-MAN GAME

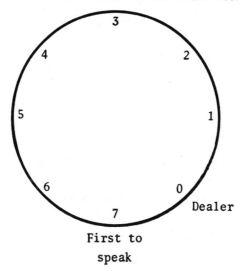

First to
speak

POSITION BEFORE THE DRAW IN A FIVE-MAN GAME

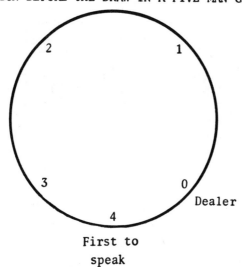

First to
speak

Numbers represent players yet to speak

Consequently, authors who describe position in this way end up also having to specify the number of players in the game. Using my convention, this difficulty is avoided.

IMPORTANT CONCEPTS

Before going on to Chapter 2, be sure that you understand

(a) The meaning of total ante; bets in pot; pass and out.
(b) The fact that each bet is assumed to equal the limit.
(c) My convention regarding labeling of positions.
(d) The effect of position on opening requirements, calling requirements, and raising requirements.

QUESTIONS

1. If each of six players antes 50¢, what is the size of the total ante?
2. The pot contains $8. Your opponent now bets $4. How many bets are in the pot (a) before he bets, (b) after he bets?
3. You are (a) first to speak in a six-man game, (b) third to speak in an eight-man game, (c) fifth to speak in a seven-man game. In each case, what position are you in?
4. If a flat limit game and a pot limit game have the same size antes, in which game does one need the better hand to open?

Answers:

1. $3
2. (a) 2, (b) 3
3. (a) 5, (b) 5, (c) 2
4. The pot limit game, unless the flat limit game has a very large limit.

2

BEST STRATEGIES

Each time you have to make a decision, you have one best play, or strategy. This strategy should depend on what you know about your opponents. Sometimes you may know little or nothing. Other times you may know approximately what hands an opponent opens with or calls with, etc. The tables in Chapters 3, 4, 5, and 6 allow you to determine your best strategy when you know something, and also when you know nothing. Let's look at an example.

Suppose, in our game as shown in Figure 1.1, that the total ante is $4. Pam opens for the limit of $2, everyone else drops, and it is up to you. What is your best strategy? In other words, what hands should you call with? What hands should you raise with?

This is a somewhat vague question, because your best strategy depends on Pam. If she plays tight (she plays only with good hands), then you should play tight. If she plays loose, then you should play loose. More accurately, if she opens only with aces or better, then your worst calling* hand should be threes up.** If she opens with kings or better,

---

* For simplicity, we will discuss only calling strategy.

** Threes up is a hand of two pairs in which threes is the higher pair.

your worst calling hand should be aces.* In general, your worst calling hand should depend on her worst opening hand in the following fashion.

TABLE 2.1

Opener's Worst Hand	Minimum Calling Hand for Last Player to Speak
A A	3 3 2 2
K K	A A
Q Q	K K
J J	Q Q
10 10	J J
8 8	9 9
6 6	7 7
2 2	4 4*
Anything	Anything

* The requirement here is fours rather than threes because threes are too likely to be beaten before the draw.

If you know Pam's worst opening hand, you can use Table 2.1 to determine what is, in a fairly strong sense, your best possible strategy. I call such strategies *best informed strategies*. If Pam's worst opening hand is jacks, your best strategy is to call with a minimum of queens. If her worst opening hand is kings, your best strategy is to call with a minimum of aces.

Now suppose that you don't know Pam's worst opening hand. It may be possible to make a good guess, in which case you can use the table as before. But often you simply won't know how she plays. When this happens, you must make an assumption. The best assumption to make is that she plays well. In essence, you assume that she follows the correct strategy. This assumption will be right if she does

* This entry is derived as follows. The pot is offering 3 to 1 odds, so you need a 1 in 4 or 25% chance to call. With kings you only have a 19% chance (entry 18, Table 3.12), but with aces you have a 37% chance (entry 17 of the same table). Therefore you need at least aces.

play well, and it will also be good in an *average* sense. Some
players play tight, others play loose, but on the *average* they
play well. The most compelling reason for the assumption,
however, is that it yields strategies that cannot lose in the
long run.*

To obtain such a strategy, simply find Pam's correct strategy and plug it into the table. In the present situation, her
correct strategy is given by Table 1.3: She should open with
queens or better. Therefore plug queens into the table.
You'll find that you need at least kings to call.

In summary, Table 2.1 should be used as follows: When
you know the opener's worst hand, simply plug that hand
into the table. When you do not know his worst hand, find
out what it *should* be and then plug that into the table.

USE OF A SAMPLE TABLE

The preceding discussion pretty well summarizes how to
use the tables in Chapters 3, 4, 5, and 6. Most tables in those
chapters look like Table 2.2. Observe that Table 2.2 is the

TABLE 2.2
Typical Strategy Table

Opener's Position	Opener's Worst Hand	Minimum Calling Hand for the Last Player to Speak
	AA*	3322
	KK*	AA
7	QQ	KK
6	JJ	QQ
5	1010	JJ
4	88	99
3	66	77
2	22	44
1	Anything	Anything

˙ These entries are included in case the opener plays tighter than he should.

* This has been proven as a mathematical theorem, at least for simple cases.

same as Table 2.1 except that it has an opener's position
column added on as a convenience. This column and the
middle column form a table that gives the correct opening
strategy for pass and out Draw (compare with Table 1.3).
This means that when you are unfamiliar with the opener,
you can find his correct strategy right in Table 2.2. For
example, suppose the opener is in seventh position. If the
game is pass and out Draw, then his worst opening hand
should be queens (third row from the top, Table 2.2).
Therefore you need at least kings to call.

ADJUSTMENTS FOR POT LIMIT OR TABLE STAKES PLAY

When you use the tables in Chapters 3 and 5, it is important to remember that they are meant for flat limit
games. They must be adjusted slightly for pot limit or table
stakes.

Opening requirements in pot limit should be between one
and two notches higher than they are in flat limit. In other
words, change kings to aces, change sixes to eights, etc.
Such an adjustment is necessary because of the threat of a
pot-size bet or raise.

The most significant adjustment must be made to the
raising and reraising tables. In pot limit Draw Poker, a
minimum raising hand should have approximately an 80%
chance of being high *before the draw*. The hands listed in the
raising tables have about a 60% chance of being high. In
other words, the requirements should be tightened considerably. I will show how to obtain good raising strategies
for pot limit in Chapter 3.

Calling strategies for pot limit may be obtained as they are
for flat limit. To illustrate, suppose the game is pass and out
Draw. The total ante equals 1 bet, and an unfamiliar opener
is in seventh position. You are last to speak. In this case, the
opener's correct strategy for flat limit is to open with kings

or better (Table 3.1).* Therefore, he needs at least aces to open in pot limit. You should assume that his worst opening hand is aces, and plug that into the appropriate calling table (Table 3.5a). The answer you will get is that you need at least jacks up to call.

DETERMINING AN OPPONENT'S BETTING HABITS

To profit most from the tables that will be presented, you should be able to approximately determine an opponent's betting habits. There are two basic ways of doing this. One is by direct observation, the other is by inference.

As a simple example of direct observation, consider a game of Draw in which you would like to know the worst hand your opponent opens with in a specific situation. Let's say the possibilities are jacks, queens, kings, and aces.

Observe your opponent's hands in a variety of show-downs. Let's say that, after drawing three cards, he presents queens and deuces on the first showdown. This means that he must have started with queens, since he would not have started with deuces. Hence you already know that he opens with queens. If he shows down jacks and deuces or three jacks, you will know for sure that he plays jacks. However, if he shows down jacks and kings, you won't know for sure. In general, if you do not see a hand like jacks and deuces or three jacks appear after a while, you should assume he does not play jacks.

Unfortunately, some players don't even know what they open with. It's kind of an urge with them. Nevertheless, if they open with a certain hand once, they will usually do so again.

Inference is a standard technique in bridge, and it can be used in poker as well. Consider, for example, an oppo-

---

* Table 1.3 indicates that he only needs queens when the total ante is 2 bets. He needs kings in this case because the total ante is smaller (1 bet).

nent who is betting unusually often. Let's say he bets about
half the time after drawing to a straight or a flush. No one
has had the guts to call him, so no one knows what he's
doing. Here the sheer mathematics of the situation says he
should only make a hand about one time in six. Consequently, if he never bluffed he would be betting about one
time in six. At present, however, he is betting about one
time in two. The inference is, therefore, that most of his
bets are probably bluffs.

As a second example, consider the player who plays every
other hand in Seven-Card Stud. We may not know exactly
what he plays, but Table 7.3 indicates that he should only
have a pair about one fifth of the time. The inference is,
therefore, that he frequently plays hands without pairs.

TELLS

The "best" strategies that I present are essentially mathematical in nature. They give excellent results while requiring
a minimum amount of information. However, because they
operate with little information, it is quite possible that even
better strategies will present themselves from time to time.
This will often happen against players whose mannerisms
give them away. For example, a player may take an extra
deep puff on his cigar whenever he has a good hand. Mannerisms of this kind are known as *tells*. Listed below are
some of the more common types.

1. *Nervous tells.*

Many players appear nervous or hesitant when their hand
is weak. This observation may be used as follows:

Suppose that your opponent has just bet $200. You say
something funny, and he breaks out into a big, natural grin.
At this point I would say that he has his bet, because it's hard
to smile when you hold nothing and hundreds of your
dollars are on the table.

You bet the pot in an early round of stud, and a timid
player calls without hesitating. Here I would expect him to
have a hand.

2. *Tells related to bet size.*

The size of a player's bet will often provide a clue to his holding. Some players bet less with bad hands and more with good ones, or vice versa. When a player gets into either of these ruts, it becomes easy to tell what he has just from the size of his bet.

3. *Tells related to the speed with which a bet is made.*

Oftentimes, a strong inference can be made from the speed with which a player bets or calls. For example, suppose in Jackpots that you raise the opener. He draws three while you draw one. After the draw he bets without hesitating. My guess here would be that he is bluffing, because the only hand that is easy to bet fast in this situation is a bust. Any reasonable hand, like trips, presents a real problem as to whether one should check it or bet, and most players (in my experience) tend to pause in this situation when they make such hands.

4. *Tells relating to a player's interest in the pot.*

Many players indicate that they intend to play before it is their turn because they show too much interest in the pot. Watch for players who sit up in their chairs, or get their chips ready ahead of time. Some players ask questions like "Whose turn is it?" Others demand to see an upcard which has already been folded.

After the draw, a player will often appear disgusted or even fold out of turn when he fails to improve. When this player does not fold out of turn, he may well have a hand.

5. *Tells based on an opponent's level.*

A player who pretends to be weak when he is strong and vice versa is said to be using one level. A player who pretends to be weak when he is weak, etc., is said to be using two levels. Many players use a particular level much more than the other. These players may be easily read in many situations. For example, suppose that your opponent is a one-level player. If he draws two cards in Jackpots (a show of strength), he probably has a pair with a kicker. Similarly, if he raises on the first round in Five-Card Stud (also a show of strength), he probably doesn't have a pair.

IMPORTANT CONCEPTS

Before going on to Chapter 3, you should understand

(a) The meaning of tell.
(b) How to use Table 2.1.
(c) How to determine opponent's betting habits.

PROBLEMS ──

1. Your opponent in a Draw Poker game shows down QQ66, AAJJ, and KK. In each case he opened in seventh position and then drew three cards. What can you say about his opening habits?

2. In a fairly loose Draw Poker game, you have observed that Fred seems to be playing every other hand. Can you say anything about what hands he is likely to be playing?

3. Joe is a very nervous player. When his hands tremble, or he hesitates before calling, it is invariably because he has a weak hand. In Five-Card Stud, you hold 8K and bet. Joe hesitates, then calls with ?Q. On the next round, you catch an ace, and he catches a nine. You bet again, and he now calls with confidence. What is Joe's probable hand?

4. Anne bets the limit on the first round whenever she has a good hole card. She now shows ?QKA10. You hold 22J96. Anne checked on the first round even though her queen was high on board. On the second and third rounds, she bet the limit. Now she bets again. What do you do?

5. Frank always bets quickly and confidently whenever he is bluffing. He opens and you call with aces. Both of you draw three. After the draw, he pauses for a while, apparently thinking. Now he bets. You have failed to improve. What do you do?

6. Harry is basically a one-level player. In Five-Card Stud, you bet with 99. Harry raises the pot with ?K. What do you do?

Answers:

1. He opens with queens, kings, and presumably with anything better. He may or may not open with jacks.
2. Since Fred figures to be dealt a pair approximately once every two deals, he is probably playing all pairs.
3. Two nines.
4. Call. Her failure to bet initially probably means that her hole card is low.
5. Fold. Frank would have bet more quickly if he were bluffing.
6. Call. In all probability, the raise shows weakness rather than strength.

3

WINNING STRATEGIES
FOR DRAW POKER:
THE FIRST ROUND

This chapter and the next present a winning system for most common forms of Draw Poker. Because of poker's complexity, the system does not cover all possible situations. However, it does provide the best strategy for most common situations, so that a player who follows the system will have a big edge over anyone who does not.

When trying out the system, don't walk directly into the biggest game you can find. Stay with small games until you build up your confidence, experience, and bankroll. Play in big games only when you are among friends or in a club that has a good reputation.

The system is presented primarily by way of tables. If you are interested in learning how the tables were computed, read Chapter 9 and the Appendix. The tables were not arrived at by guessing. No entry is off by more than one percent, and most entries are exact.

In order to use the tables, you must be familiar with the material in Chapters 1 and 2. Remember that the term "bet" will always refer to a limit-size bet, and that the tables are meant for flat limit. They should be adjusted for pot limit as indicated in Chapter 2.

The tables do not cover all possible size antes, but they may be used to approximate the correct strategies in almost all cases. I will show how this is done in the section on opening strategy.

Don't be discouraged by the number of tables. They cover a variety of different ante sizes and different styles of game. You only need concern yourself with the handful that apply to your game.

In order to use the tables in actual play, you may have to do a little memorizing, but the amount you memorize is up to you. Most players should be able to memorize the entire system for a particular game, but this is not essential. The system is sufficiently powerful so that even if you remember only a small part of it, you will still have an edge.

OPENING STRATEGY FOR PASS AND OUT GAMES

As was indicated in Chapter 1, a good opening strategy should depend on the size of the ante and the opener's position. When the ante is large, you stand to gain more when you win, so you can open with weaker hands. Conversely, when the ante is small you should wait for a good hand.

In a pass and out game your position determines the number of players left against you when it is your turn to speak. Therefore, if you have good position you will have fewer players to compete with, so you can open with weaker hands.

The effects of pot odds and position are quite evident in Table 3.1. Notice that the requirements are looser when the ante is larger, and that they decrease as your position improves.

To illustrate the use of Table 3.1, suppose your game has a limit of $8 and a total ante of $8, or a limit of $1 and a total ante of $1, or a limit of 10¢ and a total ante of 10¢. In all these cases the total ante equals 1 bet.* Therefore, in all

---

* As already indicated, the assumption is that each bet equals the limit. In the calling section of this chapter, I will explain how this assumption may be relaxed.

TABLE 3.1
Opening Strategy for
a Pass and Out Game

Minimum Opening Requirements

Players Yet to Speak	Total Ante Equals One Bet	Total Ante Equals Two Bets
7	KK	QQ or any four flush*
6	KK	JJ or any four flush
5	QQ	10 10 or any four flush
4	10 10	88 or any four flush
3	77	66 or any four flush
2	44	22 or any four flush
1	K	Anything

* It will also be right to open with high open-end straights like KQ J 10.

these cases you should use the middle column of the table. This column says that you need at least queens to open in fifth position.

Now suppose that your game has a limit of $8 and a total ante of $16, or a limit of $1 and a total ante of $2, or a limit of 10¢ and a total ante of 20¢. In all these cases the total ante equals 2 bets. Therefore, in all these cases you should use the column on the right. This column says that you need at least a pair of tens or any four flush* to open in fifth position. (Note that the requirements are reduced because the total ante is larger.)

*The logic behind opening with a four flush is as follows. After you open, one of three things can happen: You can win the ante without a contest, one or more players can call, or you can be raised. In the first case you win 2 bets. In the second case you lose slightly, on the average, if only one player calls, but you break even if two players call. To see this, simply note that when two players call the pot will be offering you odds of 4 to 1. The odds against your making a flush are also approximately 4 to 1. This means that you break roughly even when two players call. When you are raised, you figure to lose slightly over half a bet, but losses of this type are more than made up for by the 2 bets you occasionally win. In other words, your gains outweigh your losses, so you gain by opening. (For those who are interested, a more precise argument is given in Section 1 of the Appendix.)

Finally, suppose your game has a limit of $8 and a total ante of $12, or a limit of $1 and a total ante of $1.50, or a limit of 10¢ and a total ante of 15¢. In all these cases the total ante equals $1\frac{1}{2}$ bets. Your correct strategy lies somewhere between the middle column and the right-hand column. More specifically, if you are in fifth position your minimum opening hand should lie between queens and tens. In other words, it should be jacks. Such an approximation can always be made when the total ante in your game is not exactly equal to either 1 or 2 bets.

It is important to realize that Table 3.1 need not be memorized unless it applies to your game. For example, there is no point in memorizing Table 3.1 if you are playing Jackpots. Also, when the table does apply, it will only be necessary to remember one column. For instance, if your game has a total ante of 2 bets, you need only memorize the column on the right.

PROBLEM (very hard) ──────────────────────────

A popular poker book recommends that the player in first position have at least an ace-king to open if the total ante is 1 bet, and that the player in zeroth position require at least a pair of sevens to call. This advice is incorrect. Why?

Answer: If the player in zeroth position only calls or raises with sevens or better, he will be dropping roughly two times out of three (Table 3.9). If he drops two times out of three, his opponent will gain by betting with anything. However, the above advice tells his opponent to bet only with an ace-king or better. This means that the advice must be incorrect for at least one of the players.

The correct strategy for each player depends on what he knows about his opponent. If the players know nothing, their best strategies are given by Tables 3.1 and 3.5a. The best strategy for the player in first position is to open with a king or better, and the best strategy for his opponent is to call (or raise) with an ace or better.

Adjustments for Ante and Straddle Games

Most Draw games require an equal ante from each player, but there is no real reason for this. Instead of eight players each anteing 25¢, the dealer could ante $2. This is fair since the deal rotates. After each player has dealt once, everyone will have anted the same amount.

Ante and Straddle games are a special form of "unequal ante" game commonly played in clubs. In these games the player in first position (the Ante) and the player in zeroth position (the Straddle) are the only players to ante. Typically, the Ante puts in 1 chip and the Straddle puts in 2 chips. Figure 3.1 shows the seating arrangement in an eight-man Ante and Straddle game and the number of chips anted by each player.

If the uneven ante were the only significant difference between an Ante and Straddle game and an ordinary game,

FIGURE 3.1
Position in an Eight-Man Ante and Straddle Game

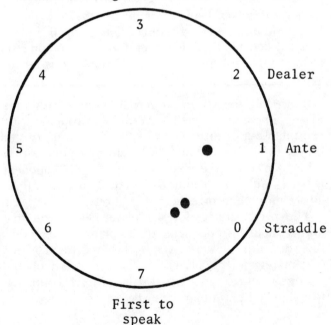

First to
speak

we could use the same strategies for both. There is another difference, however. When it comes time for either the Ante or the Straddle to act, the money he has put in the pot is considered to be part of any bet, call, or raise he may decide to make. In other words, if the bet were 4 chips and the Straddle put in 2 chips initially, then he could call for 2 additional chips, or raise for 6. Similarly, if the Ante put in 1 chip initially, he could call for 3 additional chips, or raise for 7.

TABLE 3.2
Opening Strategy for an Ante and
Straddle Game with a Total Ante
of Slightly Less Than One Bet*

Players Yet to Speak	Minimum Opening Requirements
7	A A
6	K K
5	Q Q
4	J J
3	9 9
2	7 7
1	A

* This table is meant specifically for a game that has a total ante of 3 chips and a limit of 4 chips. However, it may also be used for games that have a limit of only 3 chips.

This additional rule has the effect of reducing the amount of money that the opener stands to win whenever he is called or raised by the Ante or Straddle. As a result, the opener stands to win slightly less on the average by opening, so he needs a slightly better hand to do so.

The following table gives the correct opening strategy for Ante and Straddle games. It is applicable to games where the Ante puts in 1 chip, the Straddle puts in 2 chips, and the limit is either 3 or 4 chips.

Expected Gain from Opening Correctly

Although it might seem that the average player would continue to improve his opening, calling, and raising strategies over the years until they became nearly perfect, my experience is that many players continue for years to use strategies that are quite inaccurate. This is simply because it is very difficult to decide whether certain questionable plays are right or wrong on the basis of experience. For example, in order for a player to determine whether a certain questionable hand is profitable to open with in a certain position, he must (a) open the hand in that position many times (this in itself might take a year), (b) remember how much he won or lost on each occasion, and (c) somehow mentally weigh together all of the results so as to reach a conclusion.

So many inaccuracies creep into such a process that it is often impossible for a good player to sense when he is following a strategy that is way off. As a result, it is not uncommon to have a situation in which one intelligent player follows the right strategies and ends up winning $200 per game, whereas another equally intelligent player follows the wrong strategies and ends up losing $50.

The following table allows us to estimate how much a player can gain per year in a large game if he follows Table 3.1 or 3.2 rather than his usual strategy. The table was computed using techniques outlined in Section 1 of the Appendix. It assumes that the player has average position (he is in third position). The total ante was assumed to be $40 and the limit $20. Games with approximately these proportions may be found in most metropolitan areas.

Table 3.3 indicates that a player loses $100 per year by failing to open with sixes in third position. If he follows the advice of one book and does not open with sixes, sevens, eights, nines, and tens, he will lose $100 + $200 + $300 + $450 + $600 = $1,650 per year, just from the mistakes he makes in third position. If he makes similar types of mistakes in several other positions, he will lose at least $5,000 a year just by opening incorrectly.

TABLE 3.3
Expected Gain from Opening Correctly
When the Total Ante Equals Two Bets

If in third position you open with	Your approximate gain per year by opening with that hand in third position will be
QQ	$900*
JJ	$750
10 10	$600
99	$450
88	$300
77	$200
66	$100

* These figures assume that (a) you play two nights a week, or equivalently, you open fifty times per year with each of the hands listed; (b) your game is large ($40 total ante, $20 limit); and (c) your opponents are good players who know approximately how you play.

Before leaving this subject, I should stress that the above discussion assumes that (a) the player plays two nights a week and (b) he plays in a large game. If your game has a total ante of $4, a limit of $2, and you only play one night a week (for six hours), then the average player in your game may be able to make $250 more per year if he merely opens correctly.

OPENING STRATEGY FOR JACKPOTS

The rules of Jackpots require that one must have jacks or better to open. Sandbagging is allowed. The main advantage of sandbagging is that you can raise if anyone opens. You also avoid having to speak first after the draw. (The player who opens the pot must speak first.) The main disadvantage is that the hand may get passed out and you lose the antes. For this reason it is generally unwise to sandbag when the total ante is large (2 or more bets). It is also unwise to sandbag in a mediocre or good position (position four or less) because in this case you run too great a risk that the hand will be passed out.

An important sandbagging consideration is the number of high cards in your hand. When you hold a hand like AAAKK, for example, you cannot expect any of your opponents to open with a pair of aces or with aces up, and it is very unlikely that anyone will be able to open with kings or with kings up. As a result, the pot won't be opened that often after you check and it is therefore better for you to open.

Opening Strategy for Games with a Total Ante of One Bet

Table 3.4a illustrates the preceding points. This table indicates that sandbagging should be avoided in positions four through zero. Although I don't make it clear in the table, the only hands that are really advantageous to check in positions five, six, and seven are small and medium two pairs. All other hands of opening quality are rather border-line. I prefer to open with jacks up through aces up and with three jacks through three aces, because the high cards in these hands make it less likely that someone else will be able to open.

TABLE 3.4a
Opening Strategy for a Jackpots Game
with a Total Ante of One Bet

Players Yet to Speak	Opening Hands
7	KK, JJ22—AAKK, JJJ—AAA*
6	KK, JJ22—AAKK, JJJ—AAA
5	KK, JJ22—AAKK, JJJ—AAA
4	KK or better
3	QQ or better
2	JJ or better
1	JJ or better
0	JJ or better

* See text for explanation.

TABLE 3.4b
Opening Strategy for a Jackpots Game
with a Total Ante of Two Bets

Players Yet to Speak	Opening Hands
7	QQ or better*
6	JJ or better
5	JJ or better
4	JJ or better
3	JJ or better
2	JJ or better
1	JJ or better
0	JJ or better

* Sandbag only in seventh position and only with a hand of three deuces or better in which all five cards are below a jack.

There are two reasons for opening with kings in positions five, six, and seven. First, by opening you make slightly more, on the average, than you do by checking and then calling.* Second, you motivate your opponents to call with hands like aces and two small pairs. If you only bet with jacks up through aces up and with three jacks through three aces, your opponents would stop calling with less than queens or kings up. This would drastically reduce your profits from betting.

The rather stiff requirement of kings in fourth position is due to the fact that your opponents in fifth, sixth, and seventh positions are still threats after they pass. However, if these players never sandbag (or if your game is short-handed), then you should open with jacks in fourth position (Table 3.1).

* For the benefit of those who are mathematically inclined, the argument is as follows: By opening, you figure to make slightly over .11 of a bet (see Section 1 of the Appendix). If you check, the only way you can profit is if someone opens in a good position with possibly jacks, you call, and no one raises. The probability of this occurring is about .30. Your chances in this case will be slightly less than .40. Hence your expected gain by checking is slightly less than $.30[.40(3) - 1] = .06$

you get to play   you win   you put in

of a bet. This means that you do somewhat better by opening.

Opening Strategy for Games with a Total Ante of Two Bets

Table 3.4b gives a good opening strategy for games with a total ante of 2 bets. Because of the large ante in these games, sandbagging should generally be avoided. The only time it is right to sandbag is when you are in seventh position and you hold a good hand in which all cards are below a jack. (Possession of all low cards makes it more likely that someone else will be able to open.)

Sandbagging Errors

The following deal is an example of the kinds of sandbagging errors that are common even in professional games. It occurred in Gardena, California, some years ago. The action has been reconstructed in the tables below.

Hands Dealt

Position	Player Name	
7	A	-----*
6	B	QQQ JJ
5	C	-----
4	D	99972
3	E	AAAA3
2	F	-----
1	G	-----
0	H	KKJ52

* Worthless.

Betting Summary

A	Check	Fold				
B	Check	Raise	Raise	Raise	Raise	Call
C	Check	Fold				
D	Check	Raise	Call	Call	Call	Call
E	Check	Call	Raise	Raise	Raise	
F	Check	Fold				
G	Check	Fold				
H	Open	Fold				

Observe that both B and D make errors by not opening. B has too many high cards in his hand; D does not have enough players behind him who might open. E's check is a very bad error. He was guaranteed to win at least 20 bets on this hand as long as he opened the pot. By checking, he made the odds about 6 to 4 that he wouldn't win anything. If this hand were repeated many times, his play would cost him on the average about 12 bets.

D made an error later on by not dropping after B's second raise. B was unlikely to be bluffing in this situation, and E had already shown great strength by checking and then calling a double raise. D's failure to drop cost him 4 bets.

In short, approximately 16 bets were "blown" on this deal.

Because there is a lot of material in this chapter, it may be best to take a break at this point. Play with friends for small stakes and concentrate on opening correctly. Also, watch and see how your opponents open. You may find that their play varies depending on whether they are ahead or behind. Once you have learned the correct opening strategy for your game, you can move on to the next section.

CALLING STRATEGY BEFORE THE DRAW

Against One Opponent

We have already discussed calling strategy at some length in Chapter 2. As you may recall, your strategy should depend on the strength of the opener's hand. If the opener has bad position, he figures to have a better hand, so you should have a better hand to call. We did not discuss your position in Chapter 2, but it is also important. When you have bad position you need a better hand than you would ordinarily because of the threat from players behind you.

Tables 3.5a and 3.5b illustrate these points. I haven't explained the use of these tables yet, but notice that the requirements in any column go down as the opener's hands weaken (his position improves). Also, the requirements in any row go down (or remain the same) as your position improves. Finally, note the effect of pot odds: The require-

TABLE 3.5a
Minimum Calling Hands Against One
Opponent When the Total Ante Equals One Bet

Opener's Position	Opener's Worst Hand	6	5	4	3	2	1	0
					Your Position			
	AA**	KK22*	QQ22*	QQ22*	QQ22*	QQ22*	JJ22	JJ22
7	KK	JJ22*	101022*	8822	7722	6622	AA	AA
6	KK		101022*	8822	7722	6622	AA	AA
5	QQ			AA	AA	AA	AA	AA
4	1010				AA*	KK	KK	QQ
3	77					QQ	JJ	1010
2	44						99	77
1	K							A

* Minimum raising hand; inferior hands should be dropped.

** The row containing this entry is included in case an opponent opens with a minimum of aces.

TABLE 3.5b
Minimum Calling Hands Against One
Opponent When the Total Ante Equals Two Bets*

Opener's Position	Opener's Worst Hand	6	5	4	3	2	1	0
					Your Position			
	AA**	9922	9922	8822	8822	7722	6622	3322
	KK**	6622	AA	AA	AA	AA	AA	AA
7	QQ	AA	AA	AA	KK	KK	KK	KK
6	JJ		AA	KK	KK	KK	QQ	QQ
5	1010			KK	QQ	QQ	QQ	JJ
4	88				QQ	JJ	1010	99
3	66					1010	99	77
2	22						66	44
1	Anything							Anything

* The entries in this table were computed assuming that the opener does not open with four straights or four flushes. If he does, the requirements should be reduced slightly.

** The row containing this entry is included in case an opponent opens with a minimum of aces (kings).

ments in Table 3.5b are looser because the total ante is larger.

To see how these tables should be used, let's look at Table 3.5b. It is just an expanded version of the calling table (Table 2.2) presented in Chapter 2. Instead of just one calling column for the last player to speak (the player in position zero), we now have calling columns for the players in positions six, five, four, three, two, one, and zero. Each player should use the column that corresponds to his position. For example, a player in position one should use the column with the "1" at the top. Once the correct column has been chosen, it may be used in the same fashion as the rightmost column of Table 2.2.

As an illustration, suppose the correct column to use is the one with the "3" at the top (you're in third position). Let's say you put the opener on queens or better. In this case you should look for the entry in your column that is directly across from the entry of QQ in the "opener's worst hand" column. This entry is KK. It says that you need at least kings to call. If you had put the opener on kings or better, you would need at least aces.

FIGURE 3.2
Use Your Opponent's Worst Opening Hand
to Determine Your Correct Strategy

Opener's Position	Opener's Worst Hand	Your Position 3
	AA	8822
	KK	AA
7	QQ.....................KK
6	JJ	KK
5	1010	QQ
4	88	QQ

When you don't know your opponent's worst opening hand, you should assume that he plays well. Find what his worst opening hand *should* be, then plug that into the table.

For example, if your opponent is in fourth position in a Jackpots game, his worst opening hand should be jacks. Therefore you should use the entry in your column that is directly across from the entry "JJ" in the "opener's worst hand" column. This entry is "KK."

Expected Gain from Calling Correctly

The fact that most players make calling errors should be evident from looking at Tables 3.5a and b. Anyone who follows a strategy less complicated than the strategies in those tables must necessarily be making at least small mistakes.

Besides the simple calling errors made against one opponent, there are also errors made against two or more opponents, and errors made after the pot is raised. The average calling error before the draw in the $40 total ante, $20 limit game discussed earlier costs approximately $6. If a player makes one calling error every 15 deals and there are 45 deals per hour, he will lose roughly $18 per hour by calling incorrectly. If he plays 12 hours a week or $52 \times 12 = 624$ hours a year, he will end up giving away roughly $18 \times 624 = \$11,232$ a year, just by calling incorrectly on the first round.

Simplified Calling Strategy

Readers who do not wish to memorize Table 3.5a or 3.5b despite the preceding statistics may find it helpful to use one of the following tables. The first two give a simplified strategy for ordinary pass and out games.* The last table gives a simplified strategy for Ante and Straddle games.

To use the tables, simply evaluate the opener's position as being either bad (positions 5, 6, and 7), mediocre (positions 3 and 4), or good (positions 1 and 2), and evaluate your position in a similar fashion. (Your position is bad if

* An ordinary game has an equal ante from each player.

you are in positions 4, 5, or 6, mediocre if you are in positions 2 or 3, and good if you are in position 1 or 0.) Then use the entry that lies in the column corresponding to your position and in the row corresponding to the opener's position.

TABLE 3.5c
Simplified Calling Strategy for an Ordinary Pass and Out Game with a Total Ante of One Bet

Opener's Position		Your Position		
		6 5 4 Bad	3 2 Mediocre	1 0 Good
7 6 5	Bad	101022*	6622	A A
4 3	Mediocre		K K	Q Q
2 1	Good	.		7 7

* Minimum raising hand. Inferior hands should be dropped.

TABLE 3.5d
Simplified Calling Strategy for an Ordinary Pass and Out Game with a Total Ante of Two Bets

Opener's Position		Your Position		
		6 5 4 Bad	3 2 Mediocre	1 0 Good
7 6 5	Bad	A A	K K	Q Q
4 3	Mediocre		J J	9 9
2 1	Good			4 4

TABLE 3.5e
Simplified Calling Strategy for an Ante and Straddle
Game with a Total Ante of Slightly Less Than One Bet

Opener's Position		6 5 4 Bad	3 2 Mediocre	1 0 Good
		Your Position		
7 6 5	Bad	QQ22*	9922	AA
4 3	Mediocre		AA	QQ
2 1	Good			22**

* Minimum raising hand; inferior hands should be dropped.
** This entry is lower than the corresponding entry in Table 3.5c because the Ante and Straddle can call for less.

For example, suppose the total ante is $4 and the opening bet is $4. The total ante is 1 bet, so you should use Table 3.5c.* If your position is good and the opener's position is mediocre, your minimum calling hand should be queens. If your position is good and the opener's position is bad, your minimum calling hand should be aces.

Calling Strategy for Jackpots

In Jackpots it is possible that a player may open with queens but sandbag with three deuces or better. In cases of this type, treat him as though he opens with queens or better. In other words, go by his worst opening hand. If you don't

---

* I assume that the game is of the ordinary pass and out variety.

know what that is, assume he follows Table 3.4b when the total ante is 2 bets and that he opens with aces or better in the worst three positions* and otherwise follows Table 3.4a when the total ante is 1 bet.

Always take sandbaggers into account when you call. If you are in second position and the players in sixth and seventh positions routinely sandbag, then you really have four active players behind you rather than two. Consequently, you should use the columns in Tables 3.5a and 3.5b that have "4" at the top.

Readers who do not wish to use Tables 3.5a or 3.5b may prefer to use Table 3.5f for 3.5g. These give a simplified calling strategy for Jackpots. They may be used in the same fashion as Tables 3.5c, d, and e.**

TABLE 3.5f
Simplified Calling Strategy for a Jackpots
Game with a Total Ante of One Bet

Opener's Position		Your Position 6 5 4 Bad	3 2 Mediocre	1 0 Good
7 6 5	Bad	QQ22*	JJ22	101022
4 3	Mediocre		6622	٦A
2 1	Good			KK

* Minimum raising hand; inferior hands should be dropped.

* This assumption is slightly conservative and leads to a somewhat conservative calling strategy.
** Tables 3.5f and 3.5g take sandbaggers into account. Therefore no adjustments are needed to use the tables.

TABLE 3.5g
Simplified Calling Strategy for a Jackpots
Game with a Total Ante of Two Bets

Opener's Position		Your Position		
		6 5 4 Bad	3 2 Mediocre	1 0 Good
7 6 5	Bad	A A	K K	K K
4 3	Mediocre		K K	K K
2 1	Good			Q Q

Calling Against Two Opponents

In general, requirements for calling should be increased slightly when there are more players in the pot. Specifically, when A opens and B calls, C should require a hand that is a notch better than the worst hand B would call with. In other words, if B's minimum is queens, C's minimum should be kings. If B's minimum is kings, C's minimum should be aces. If B's minimum is aces, C's minimum should be approximately eights and deuces.*

To use this "rule" against unfamiliar opposition, simply determine what B *should* call with, using either Table 3.5a or 3.5b, and then increase this requirement a notch. As an example, suppose your game is an ordinary pass and out with a total ante of 1 bet. Player A opens in third position and B calls in second position. You are in zeroth position. In this case B's call should indicate at least queens (Table

---

* Normally I consider threes and deuces to be a notch above aces. In this case threes and deuces are insufficient for calling purposes because they figure to be beaten before the draw and they are unlikely to improve.

3.5a, bottom entry in the "2" column). Therefore you need at least kings.

Calling Against a Player Who Has Bet Less Than the Limit*

Thus far I have assumed that players bet and raise the limit. The strategies I present require little or no adjustment to handle situations in which players bet less than the limit. To see why some adjustment may occasionally be necessary, consider a game with a total ante of $2 and a limit of $2. Ordinarily we would assume that if someone opened, he would open for the limit ($2). However, let's say someone opens for $1. Now the total ante equals 2 bets, so you should use Table 3.5b. However, this table was computed assuming that the opening bet equaled the limit (the limit was $1). In this game the limit is $2, which means that someone behind you can raise more than the table anticipated. Therefore it is possible that you may need a slightly better hand than Table 3.5b indicates.**

In these situations, follow Table 3.5b but drop hands that are very borderline. These are hands that represent a call in your present position but would represent a drop if your position were one seat worse.

The above advice assumes that you are familiar with your opponent, in which case you should go by the worst hand that he opens with for $1. When you are not familiar with your opponent, keep in mind that he may have a better hand than he would in a $1 limit game. To account for this possibility, you can credit him with a worst hand that is a notch better than usual, and then plug this hand into Table 3.5b.

---

* This section is fairly hard and can be skipped, especially if players in your game usually bet the limit.

** The same kind of statement can be made if you want to open for $1 when the total ante is $2 and the limit is $2. The right-hand column of Table 3.1 was computed assuming that the limit equaled the amount bet (the limit was $1). In this case you can get raised more than $1, so you may have to increase some of the entries in that column.

PROBLEM (hard) ——————————————————————

Two equally talented players are sitting at the table. One
plays too loose, the other too tight. Which player is more
likely to sense that something is wrong with his strategy?

Answer: The loose player must observe that hands he
plays lose money. The tight player must observe that hands
he *does not play* make money. It is easier to see that hands
you play lose money than it is to see that hands you do not
play make money. Consequently, the loose player is more
likely to sense that something is wrong with his strategy.

*Now is another good time to take a break. Play for small stakes
and concentrate on trying to open and call correctly. Since you
presumably now know the correct opening strategy, you shouldn't
have to look it up when you are unfamiliar with an opponent.
Observe how your opponents play. Insist that all active hands be
shown when a showdown occurs. Once you feel that you can open
and call reasonably well, you can move on to the next section.*

RAISING STRATEGY

Against One Opponent

The only important raising consideration is the strength
of your opponent's hand. If he opened in a bad position,
he figures to have a better hand, so you should have a better
hand to raise. Your position will generally be unimportant.
If your hand is good enough to raise with in a good position,
it will generally be good enough to raise with in all positions.
The only exception to this occurs when the total ante is
fairly small (one bet or less), and you immediately follow the
opener. In this case you may have to increase your requirements slightly (see Table 3.6a).

Tables 3.6a and 3.6b give good strategies for raising and
reraising against one opponent. They may be used in the
same fashion as Table 2.1. To illustrate: Suppose first that
you are considering raising the opener. The total ante equals

1 bet. In this case you should use Table 3.6a. If you put the opener on kings or better, your minimum raising hand should be nines and deuces (top row, Table 3.6a). If you put him on sevens or better, your minimum raising hand should be kings (fifth row from top, Table 3.6a). When you don't know his worst opening hand, assume that he plays well. If he *should* open with tens or better, then you should raise with aces or better (fourth row from the top, Table 3.6a).

Suppose now that you opened and are considering reraising. In this case you need three sevens to reraise if you

TABLE 3.6a
Raising Strategy Against One Opponent When
the Total Ante Equals One Bet

Opener's Position	Opener's Minimum Hand	Minimum Raising Hand	Minimum Reraising Hand
7	KK	9922*	777
6	KK	9922	777
5	QQ	3322**	222
4	1010	AA	KK22
3	77	KK	JJ22
2	44	QQ	8822
1	K	77	KK

* This entry should be jacks up if the raiser is in sixth position, tens up if he is in fifth position. *It should always be jacks up against a mediocre opponent.* The reason for raising with nines up against a good player is to disguise the fact that you hold two pairs. A good player will put you on two small pairs if you flat call and draw one because the total ante is not large enough to warrant your drawing to a straight or a flush. As a result, he will bet with most two pairs after the draw. This will cost you. By raising, you persuade him to check with many hands that he would otherwise have bet. Such a raise is not necessary, however, when the total ante is 2 bets because in this case your opponent may put you on a four flush or a four straight when you call. This explains why the raising requirements in the first row of Table 3.6b are tighter than they are in the third row of Table 3.6a. One other minor point: Notice that the minimum *reraising* hand against an opponent with kings or better is jacks up (third row from bottom, Table 3.6a) rather than nines up. This is because when you open and reraise you have to speak first after the draw. There is no point in reraising with nines up to show strength when you are later going to have to check and show weakness.

** This entry should be sevens up if the raiser is in third position, eights up if he is in fourth position. *It should always be eights up against a mediocre opponent.*

TABLE 3.6b
Raising Strategy Against One Opponent When
the Total Ante Equals Two Bets*

Opener's Position	Opener's Minimum Hand	Minimum Raising Hand	Minimum Reraising Hand
7	QQ	8822	666
6	JJ	3322	222
5	1010	AA	KK22
4	88	KK	JJ22
3	66	KK	JJ22
2	22	JJ	3322
1	Anything	55	QQ

* Entries were computed assuming that the opener does not open with four straights and four flushes. If he does, the requirements should be reduced slightly.

put your opponent on nines up or better (top row, Table 3.6a). You need three deuces to reraise if you put him on threes up or better (third row from top, Table 3.6a). If you don't know how he plays, assume that he plays well. If you open with tens or better in your position, you should assume that he raises with aces or better (fourth row from the top, Table 3.6a), which means that you need kings up to reraise.

Readers who do not wish to memorize the table that applies to their game may find it convenient to remember just a few of its entries and then use those to approximate the rest. For example, suppose you remember that you need aces to raise someone who has tens or better (fourth row from top, Table 3.6a) and queens to raise someone who has fours or better (sixth row from top, Table 3.6a). Then you can use this information to conclude that you need kings to raise someone who has sevens or better (fifth row from top, Table 3.6a). You can also conclude that you probably need threes and deuces to raise someone who has jacks or better, and that you probably need jacks to raise someone who has deuces or better.

Raising Against More Than One Opponent

In general, raising requirements should be increased slightly when there are more players in the pot. In other words, if A opens and B calls, the requirements for raising should be a notch higher than they would be if B wasn't in the pot. This means a requirement of kings should be changed to aces, a requirement of aces should be changed to threes up, etc.

We can get a feel for why this is necessary by looking at a typical contest. Suppose A opens with a minimum of jacks, B calls, and you hold threes and deuces. Ordinarily, with B out of the pot, you would have a borderline raise (Table 3.6b). B's mere call indicates that he *should* have less than threes and deuces. If this is the case, it can be verified mathematically that you also have a borderline raise.* The problem is that many players call in this situation with better than threes and deuces. Because B may have done so, the requirements for raising should be increased. In the present case a good raising minimum would be sevens up.

Here is another good spot to take a break. Play with friends and concentrate on opening, calling, and raising correctly. Observe how your opponents open, call, and raise. Insist that each player show his hand when a showdown occurs.

CALLING AFTER A RAISE

Once the opener is raised, a player who has not yet entered the pot must decide whether he wants to put in 2 bets** to play. In general, he should have a good hand to do so.

---

* By raising you risk 1 additional bet to win 2 additional bets. This means that you need slightly over a 1 in 3 (33%) chance of winning in a showdown in order to raise. If B has any pair aces or lower, your chances of winning in a showdown will be 37%. These chances give you a borderline raise.

** Remember that the strategies given here are meant for flat limit games. In other words, they are meant for situations in which the opener bets $2 and gets raised $2. The strategies must be tightened when the opener bets $2 and gets raised $5.

Two players, especially the raiser, have already shown strength. Furthermore, the raiser may continue to bet after the draw, so that a showdown will often cost at least 3 bets.

Tables 3.7a and 3.7b give the minimum acceptable standards for playing in these situations. When using the tables, the most important consideration should be the raiser's minimum hand. If the total ante is 1 bet and the raiser figures to have at least threes up, then a player who calls should

TABLE 3.7a
Calling Strategy If the Pot Has Been Raised
and the Total Ante Equals One Bet

Opener's Position	Opener's Minimum Hand	Raiser's Minimum Hand	Minimum Calling Hand
7	KK	9922	AA22
6	KK	9922	AA22
5	QQ	3322	QQ22
4	1010	AA	101022
3	77	KK	3322
2	44	QQ	AA
1	K	77	—*

* There is no entry here because the raiser is presumed to be in zeroth position, i.e., there is no one behind him who can call.

TABLE 3.7b
Calling Strategy If the Pot Has Been Raised
and the Total Ante Equals Two Bets

Opener's Position	Opener's Minimum Hand	Raiser's Minimum Hand	Minimum Calling Hand
7	QQ	8822	QQ22
6	JJ	3322	JJ22
5	1010	AA	9922
4	88	KK	AA
3	66	KK	AA
2	22	JJ	KK
1	Anything	55	—

have at least queens up (third row from top, Table 3.7a). When the raiser's minimum hand is not known, one can determine what it *should* be and then plug that into the table.

CALLING AFTER BEING RAISED

Another situation that occurs frequently is that the opener gets raised, in which case he has to decide whether to call. In most cases he will have to call even though it won't be profitable to do so, simply to protect himself from being bluffed out by garbage. For example, suppose the total ante equals 2 bets and the opener gets raised by Bill, who we assume has good position. Bill is risking 2 bets to win 3: the opener's, plus the 2 bets in the total ante. Therefore, if the opener drops half the time, Bill will profit by raising with anything. From the opener's viewpoint, he may not want to call over half the time, but he has to if Bill is prone to bluffing.

My experience is that most players fall into one of two categories, those who bluff before the draw and those who don't. Tables 3.8a and 3.8b give the correct strategy against a single opponent who *doesn't bluff*. These tables should be

TABLE 3.8a
Minimum Calling Hands After Being Raised
When the Total Ante Equals One Bet

Your Position	Your Minimum Opening Hand	Raiser's Minimum Hand	Minimum Calling Hand*
7	KK	9922	JJ22
6	KK	9922	JJ22
5	QQ	3322	8822
4	1010	AA	3322
3	77	KK	AA
2	44	QQ	KK
1	K	77	88

* See text for explanation.

TABLE 3.8b
Minimum Calling Hands After Being Raised
When the Total Ante Equals Two Bets

Your Position	Your Minimum Opening Hand	Raiser's Minimum Hand	Minimum Calling Hand
7	QQ	8822	101022
6	JJ	3322	7722
5	1010	AA	3322
4	88	KK	AA
3	66	KK	AA
2	22	JJ	QQ
1	Anything	55	66

followed unless your opponent bluffs over one time in ten, in which case you should call with everything except possibly two small pairs. These hands have only a one in eleven chance of improving and therefore do not warrant a call if your opponent figures to have them beat.

Note that the minimum calling hand in Tables 3.8a and 3.8b is always roughly a notch higher than the raiser's minimum hand. This observation can be used to minimize the amount of effort required to memorize either table.

DECEPTIVE PLAYS

It frequently happens in Jackpots that you will open with jacks or queens and one player will call. A good deceptive play in this situation is to draw one card as though you had two pairs or three of a kind, and then bet after the draw. If your opponent drops, you will have succeeded in bluffing him out, since his call indicated that he could beat your hand. If he calls, he will remember your play, and he will also call you when you do have two pairs or three of a kind. If you never make this play, your opponents will always put you on a minimum of two pairs when you open and draw one, and they will be right.

Two deceptive draws that should almost always be made are a one-card draw to three of a kind and a three-card draw to a pairless hand. Drawing four cards is simply too weak, and has about the same chance of winning as drawing three. Drawing one card to three of a kind disguises the hand. Of course, rapping pat* with three of a kind, or even with two high pairs, is often a good play. These hands don't figure to improve, and if you have gotten caught several times rapping pat as a bluff, this type of play should be very effective.

My favorite complete bluff is to open and then rap pat. I then bet after the draw as though I had a straight or a flush. This play insures my getting some calls when I do have straights and flushes, and when not overdone it makes money by itself. Another good complete bluff is to flat call and then rap pat. However, in order to get away with this type of bluff, you must occasionally flat call when you really do have a pat hand.

The following problem occurred in actual play.

PROBLEM

Your opponent in a Jackpots game likes to sandbag in his position. He opens, and you raise with aces up. He now reraises and you call. You draw one and miss. He raps pat. The limit was $5 before the draw and is now $10. He bets the limit. What do you do?

Answer: It is unlikely that your opponent would reraise with a low three of a kind and then rap pat. With any better hand, he might have sandbagged. Hence a call is in order.

You have now essentially completed Chapter 3. If you have absorbed most of the material, you should be able to play nearly perfectly on the first round. Play for small stakes and practice using the strategies in this chapter. Don't be discouraged if you lose once or twice since you still haven't learned the correct strategy for playing after the draw and it takes a while to get to know one's opponents. Do not play in a game where the operator takes a large

* By "rapping pat" a player indicates that he will not draw any cards.

percentage out of each pot. If he's charging you a reasonable amount to play, he should be willing to charge you by the hour so you know exactly how much you're paying.

MATHEMATICAL TABLES

This section is included for the benefit of mathematically minded readers and may be skipped. It contains tables that were used repeatedly to compute the strategies given in this chapter.

Table 3.9 is essentially a list of the various common poker hands and their probabilities of being dealt. As an illustra-

TABLE 3.9
Chances in 520 of Being Dealt Certain Hands

1	Full house or better
2	Flush or better
4	Straight or better
10	Three eights or better
15	Three deuces or better
21	KK55 or better
27	JJ33 or better
33	8877 or better
40	3322 or better
57	AA or better
74	KK or better
91	QQ or better
108	JJ or better
125	1010 or better
142	99 or better
159	88 or better
176	77 or better
193	66 or better
210	55 or better
227	44 or better
244	33 or better
261	22 or better
361	A or better
428	K or better
471	Q or better

tion of its use, suppose you're playing pot limit and you figure the opener for jacks or better. If you want to raise the pot, you shouldn't have more than one chance in five of being beaten before the draw. Consequently, since a pair of jacks is hand number 108 in the table, your minimum raising hand should be hand number $108/5 \approx 21$, or roughly kings up. As a second example, suppose the opener figures to have kings or better. Kings are hand number 74, so now you need at least hand number $74/5 \approx 15$, which is three deuces. In flat limit you would only need nines up.

The next table, 3.10, is particularly useful since it tells you what the chances are that someone else will have a better hand. To illustrate, suppose that you are considering opening in seventh seat with kings. The entry of 42% across from the K K and under the 7 indicates that you have close to an even chance of having the best hand at the table. Therefore

TABLE 3.10
Chances of Having Been Dealt the Best Hand

	Number of Opponents						
Your Hand	1	2	3	4	5	6	7
2 2 2	97%	94%	92%	89%	87%	84%	82%
K K 7 7	96%	92%	88%	85%	81%	78%	75%
J J 10 10	95%	90%	86%	81%	77%	73%	69%
9 9 8 8	94%	88%	83%	78%	73%	69%	65%
7 7 3 3	93%	86%	80%	74%	68%	63%	59%
A A	92%	85%	78%	72%	66%	61%	56%
K K	88%	78%	69%	61%	54%	48%	42%
Q Q	85%	72%	61%	52%	44%	37%	32%
J J	82%	67%	55%	45%	37%	30%	25%
10 10	78%	61%	47%	37%	29%	22%	17%
9 9	75%	56%	42%	31%			
8 8	72%	52%	37%	27%			
7 7	68%	46%	31%				
6 6	65%	42%	27%				
5 5	62%	38%	24%				
4 4	58%	34%	20%				
3 3	55%	30%	17%				
2 2	52%	27%	14%				

you should definitely open if the total ante equals two bets, because you're getting 2 to 1 odds on an almost even-money proposition. When the total ante is 1 bet, the situation is much closer, but it turns out that it's still right to open. (See Section 1 of the Appendix for an explanation.)

TABLE 3.11
Probability of Winning in a Variety of Contests

Entry	Hand 1	Hand 2
1	KK 78%	QQ or any lower pair 22%
2	JJ22 78%*	QQ or any higher pair 26%
3	JJ22 82%	66 or any pair between 1010 and 33 18%
4	KK22 88%	QQ or any pair between QQ and 33 12%
5	KK22 91%	QQ33 or any lower two pairs 9%
6	333 88%	QQ or any pair above threes 12%
7	22 66%	A 34%
8	1010 82%	A 18%
9	66 69%	KJ 31%
10	88 71%	KJ 29%
11	88 73%	K 27%
12	44 66%	K 34%

* Probability of winning in a showdown.

TABLE 3.11 (Continued)
Probability of Winning in a Variety of Contests

Entry	Hand 1	Hand 2	Hand 3	Hand 4
13	A 60%	K 40%		
14	K 58%	J10 42%		
15	K 58%	7 42%		
16	AA 59%	KK 21%	QQ 20%	
17	JJ22 54%	KK 24½%	QQ 21½%	
18	AA22 76½%	KK 12½%	QQ 11%	
19	333 80%	JJ44 9%	AA 11%	
20	KK22 66½%	QQ33 9%	AA 24½%	
21	8877 39%	KK 23%	QQ 20%	JJ 17%
22	AA22 65½%	KK 12½%	QQ 11½%	JJ 10½%

If you ever want to know your chances of beating various other hands, Table 3.11 provides that information. For example, if your opponent has a pair of tens and you have a pair of deuces, entry 1 gives you a 22% chance of ending up with the better hand after the draw. (Entry 1 applies to any contest in which one player has a higher pair than the other.) Most entries in Table 3.11, like entry 1, are more general than they would initially seem. For example, entry 18 would be virtually unchanged if hand 2 were a pair of tens, hand 3 were a pair of fives, etc.

TABLE 3.12
Probability of Winning Against a Player
Whose Worst Likely Hand Is Known

Entry	Your Hand	Opponent's Hand	Probability of Your Winning in a Showdown
1	AA22	9922 or better	49%
2	KK22	9922 or better	37%
3	8822	9922 or better	8%
4	AA	9922 or better	18%
5	QQ22	3322 or better	42%
6	JJ22	3322 or better	37%
7	AA	3322 or better	19%
8	QQ	3322 or better	16%
9	KK22	AA or better	58%
10	101022	AA or better	40%
11	9922	AA or better	37%
12	3322	AA or better	28%
13	KK	AA or better	19%
14	99	AA or better	15%
15	101022	KK or better	50%
16	3322	KK or better	39%
17	AA	KK or better	37%
18	KK	KK or better	19%
19	3322	QQ or better	46%
20	AA	QQ or better	46%
21	KK	QQ or better	33½%
22	JJ	QQ or better	19%
23	3322	JJ or better	50%
24	AA	JJ or better	53%
25	QQ	JJ or better	29%
26	AA	1010 or better	57%
27	QQ	1010 or better	37%
28	1010	77 or better	37%
29	22	77 or better	20%
30	77	66 or better	27%
31	QQ	44 or better	57%
32	66	22 or better	36%

The following important observations may be made from Table 3.11:

1. An inferior hand typically has about a 20% chance of winning.
2. If there are several people in the pot and you have an inferior hand, your chances of winning will be about the same as your chances of beating the best hand going in. (For example, the worst hand has a 22% chance in entry 1, a 20% chance in entry 16.)
3. It is often mathematically right to keep two high cards instead of drawing four cards (compare entries 10 and 11).

Table 3.12 was computed using Tables 3.9 and 3.11. It gives your chances of beating a player whose worst likely hand is known. For example, if the opener figures to have tens or better and you have aces, then entry 26 gives you a 57% chance of winning in a showdown. This means that you have a borderline raise (Rule 9.3, Chapter 9).

4

WINNING STRATEGIES
FOR DRAW POKER:
THE SECOND ROUND

Until now we have only been concerned with the correct strategies before the draw. As we shall see, the situation changes considerably after the draw. The tables in this chapter look different, and they are also used somewhat differently. I will explain how the tables should be used as they are presented.

READING HANDS

The basic idea behind reading hands is to consider your opponent's actions before the draw and the number of cards he took, and then try to form a picture of his probable hand. This type of analysis is a prerequisite to making good plays after the draw.

An opponent who took one card virtually always has two pairs, three of a kind, or a four flush or four straight. If he called initially in a situation where he was getting pot odds of less than 3 to 1, his most likely hand is a low two pairs. If he raised he is more likely to have a high two pairs or three of a kind, but a low two pairs is also a possibility. When an opponent may have any two pairs or three of a kind, the odds are 25 to 11 that he will have two pairs.

A player who draws two cards figures to have a pair plus a high kicker, especially if he merely called in the opening round. Ironically, such a draw tends to show weakness rather than strength, because it usually indicates a *low* pair.

Three-card draws present no problems. However, it is useful to realize that a player in a bad position who draws three cards figures to have aces or kings.

Someone who raps pat may be doing so on a complete bluff, with a legitimate pat hand, or with a high two pairs or three of a kind. In general, a player who raised and rapped pat is much more likely to be bluffing than one who merely called. The important thing to realize is that a player only figures to be dealt a pat hand about 1 time in 130. Consequently, if you see someone rap pat several times in one night, you can be fairly sure he has attempted at least one pat bluff.

GENERAL STRATEGY

Any decision to bet or raise should be preceded by an estimation of what your opponents would call you with and what they would raise you with. The fact that you are heavily favored to win does not make it right to bet. It is the proportion of times that you will be *called* and will win that counts.

A classic example of the value of this type of thinking occurs when you make three aces against an opponent who drew one card to a flush. True, your hand is quite good, but your opponent will not call with less than a flush. Consequently, you will never win when he calls, so a bet is pointless.

It is also a good idea to consider the advantages of checking before you bet. For example, suppose you make a full house against a player who drew to a flush. If he always raises with a straight or flush when someone bets into him, then you should bet so he will raise and you can reraise. However, if he never raises when someone bets into him, then you should check so you can raise later.

Table 4.1 may be useful in determining the wisdom of betting or raising after the draw. For example, suppose your single opponent drew three cards and now bets. Let's say he bets whenever he improves. Table 4.1 indicates that when he does improve, he will improve to three of a kind almost half the time.* Consequently, it would be wrong for you to raise with a high two pairs.

TABLE 4.1
Chance That an Opponent Improved
(Each Player Drew Three Cards)

Probability That an Opponent	Number of Opponents			
Made at Least	1	2	3	4
Two pairs	29%	50%	65%	76%
Three of a kind	13%	24%	34%	42%
Full house	1%	2%	3%	4%

Probability That the Best Hand Made Was				
Two pairs	16%	26%	31%	34%
Three of a kind	12%	22%	31%	38%
Full house	1%	2%	3%	4%

PAIR VERSUS PAIR CONTESTS

This section presents the correct strategies for a two-player contest in which each player has drawn three cards to a pair. We will discuss what hands they should bet with, bluff with, call with, and raise with. Other types of contests will be discussed in subsequent sections. In each contest the opener speaks first after the draw.

---

* This statement is based on column 1, which says that a single opponent will improve 29% of the time and will improve to three of a kind or better 13% of the time. Since 13% is almost half of 29%, an opponent will improve to three of a kind or better almost half of the time that he improves.

The tables in this section are applicable to either flat limit or pot limit games. They assume that someone opened and someone else called. They are not directly applicable to situations in which the pot was raised before the draw. However, such situations in which one pair raises another are quite rare.

The tables give the correct strategies for three different values of pot odds so as to cover games with different limits and ante sizes. If you play in only one game, you will probably only need to know the correct strategies for one value of pot odds. This means that you only need to remember a fraction of each table.

BETTING STRATEGY

For Opener

The basic idea behind betting strategy is that you should bet whenever you figure to make more by betting than you do by checking. Most of the time this boils down to saying that you should bet whenever it is profitable to do so. Since you only gain by betting when your opponent calls and loses, it follows that any hand you bet should be able to beat him at least half of the time when he calls. A slight safety factor is desirable, however, because of the danger of a raise. The hands listed in Table 4.2a were determined by figuring out how often your opponent should call (or raise), and then making sure that you would win at least 60% of the time when that happened.

In general, betting strategy should depend on the following two considerations: (a) the odds offered by the pot, and (b) the worst hand your opponent may have drawn to.

We have already discussed the first consideration in Chapter 1. As you may recall, when the pot offers better odds, you and your opponent should bet, call, and raise with weaker hands.

The effect of the second consideration is similar to that of the first. When your opponent is drawing weaker, he

TABLE 4.2a
Minimum Betting Hands for the Opener

Worst Hand He Opens With*	Bets in Pot		
	1	**2**	**3**
KK	AA22	3322**	3322
QQ	AA22	3322	3322
JJ	KK22	3322	3322
99	QQ22	3322	AA
66	QQ22	3322	AA
22	JJ22	3322	KK

* See explanation preceding table.

** The opener cannot make such a hand, because he is presumed to have started with at least kings. However, this is theoretically the worst hand that is profitable to bet. It should be noted that threes up is just as good as kings up when the caller figures to be drawing to aces.

will end up with weaker hands, so the hands he calls with will be weaker. This means that you can bet with weaker hands, which in turn means that he can raise with weaker hands. In other words, the betting, calling, and raising requirements should all be reduced.

Notice in Table 4.2a that the strategies are given in terms of the worst hand that you would ordinarily open with in your position, rather than in terms of the worst hand your opponent may have drawn to. This was done for the sake of convenience. The worst hand you open with should determine the worst hand he calls with (Tables 3.5a and b), which is also the worst hand that he draws to. Consequently, by specifying the worst hand that you open with, we indirectly specify his minimum drawing hand.

To see how Table 4.2a should be used, suppose the pot contains $20 and the limit is $20, or the pot contains $4 and the limit is $4, or the pot contains 50¢ and the limit is 50¢. In all these cases the pot contains 1 bet. If you open with kings or better in your present position, you should use the row that has "KK" as its leftmost entry. This is the

FIGURE 4.1
Your Correct Strategy Is Determined by the Number of Bets in the Pot and by the Worst Hand that You Open With in Your Present Position

Worst Hand He Opens With		Bets in Pot	
	1	2	3
KK...............AA22		3322	3322
QQ AA22		3322	3322
JJ KK22		3322	3322

top row. It says that your minimum betting hand should be aces up.

If the pot contained $40 and the limit was $20, or the pot contained $8 and the limit was $4, the pot would contain 2 bets and you would only need threes and deuces. You would also need threes and deuces if the pot contained 3 bets. Note that you can reduce your requirements as the pot gets larger.

Table 4.2a should be followed in general, but there are situations when it will pay you to modify your strategy somewhat. For example, since your gain by betting with a specific hand depends on how frequently your opponent calls, it follows that you may do better by checking with a borderline hand if he calls less than he should. (How to spot such players will be discussed in the section on bluffing.) Also, if your opponent tends to bet frequently after you check, it may be more profitable for you to check with a really good hand.

PROBLEM

Alice opens with jacks, and George calls. They both draw three. Alice makes jacks up. One book claims that Alice should check at this point because George will not call unless he improves. The size of the pot was not mentioned. Why is this advice poorly founded?

Answer: The argument rests on the assumption that George will drop 71% of the time (Table 4.1). If he does this, he will leave himself wide open for a bluff.

Betting Strategy for the Second Player to Speak

The second player to speak should bet any hand that figures to win over half the time when the opener calls. Table 4.2b was computed by figuring out how often the opener should call, and then making sure that the second player would win at least half the time when that happened.

In order to use Table 4.2b, simply determine the worst hand you would ordinarily draw to in your present situation. (This is the same as the worst hand you would ordinarily call with before the draw.) If you wouldn't have drawn to less than queens, use the row that has "QQ" as its leftmost entry. This row says that your minimum betting hand should be threes and deuces when the pot contains 1 or 2 bets, and aces when the pot contains 3 bets.

Note that the second player to speak can bet with weaker hands than the first player. This is because the first player shows weakness by checking.

TABLE 4.2b
Minimum Betting Hands for the Second Player to Speak

Worst Hand He Might Have Drawn To*	Bets in Pot		
	1	2	3
AA	AA22	3322	3322
KK	QQ22	3322	3322
QQ	3322	3322	AA
1010	3322	AA	KK
77	AA	KK	QQ
44	AA	QQ	JJ

* See explanation preceding table.

If you intend to memorize parts of Tables 4.2a and 4.2b, remember that for any one game it will usually suffice to know a column, or part of a column, from each table. Only the first three rows in each table apply to Jackpots.

BLUFFING STRATEGY

To illustrate some of the ideas behind bluffing strategy, suppose the game is Jackpots. You open in a good position with jacks. One opponent calls, presumably with at least queens. You fail to improve. At this point your hand is essentially hopeless: You cannot check and expect to win the pot. However, this does not necessarily mean that you should bluff—and if your opponent is getting his chips ready to call, you almost certainly should not.

Unfortunately, most players do not have obvious tells of this kind. The best you can usually hope for is to know approximately *how often* your opponent drops in a particular situation. He should drop in such a fashion that you approximately break even in the long run by bluffing. If he drops more than he should, you will gain by bluffing and should bluff with any hopeless hand. If he drops less than he should, you will lose by bluffing and should bluff as little as possible without being obvious.

Whether your opponent "overdrops" or "underdrops" can often be determined by comparing the fraction of time that he drops to the fraction of time that he should drop, which is given by Rule 9.4 of Chapter 9. This rule essentially says that he should drop in such a fashion that the odds against your winning by bluffing equal your pot odds. This way he insures that you break even, on the average, by bluffing. If the pot contains 2 bets and you are considering bluffing, then the pot is offering you 2 to 1 odds, so he should call (or raise) twice for every time that he drops. (He should call or raise two-thirds of the time, and drop one-third of the time.) By calling in this fashion, he insures that you break even by bluffing since you're getting 2 to 1 odds on a 2 to 1 bet. If he calls (or raises) less than two-thirds of the time, he is dropping too much and you will gain by bluffing with any hopeless hand.

An alternative approach for determining whether your opponent overcalls or undercalls is to compare the hands that he calls with to the hands that he should call with. (The hands that he should call with are given in Tables 4.4a and 4.4b.) For example, if Table 4.4b indicates that he should call (raise) with queens or better but he never calls with less than aces, he is dropping too much.

When you don't know how your opponent plays, you should still bluff, but you shouldn't bluff too much or too little. If you bluff too much, a good player will call with hands like aces and kings and your bluffs will end up costing you. Similarly, if you bluff too little, a good player will stop calling with less than queens up and your profit by betting legitimately will go down.

If you bluff "just right" it won't matter whether your opponent calls with hands like aces or not. This will happen when the odds against your bet being a bluff equal his pot odds. In other words, if he's getting 3 to 1 odds after you bet, then you should bluff 1 time for every 3 times that you bet legitimately.

Tables 4.3a and 4.3b were designed so that if you bet according to Tables 4.2a and 4.2b, and bluff according to Tables 4.3a and 4.3b, you will be bluffing "just right," and the hands you will be bluffing with will be your worst ones.

As an example of using Tables 4.3a and 4.3b, suppose you normally open with queens or better in your position. In this case you should use the row in Table 4.3a that has "QQ" as its leftmost entry. This row says that your *best* bluffing hand should be QQ1098 when the pot contains 1 or 2 bets, and QQ987 when the pot contains 3 bets.

As second to speak, determine your strategy by using the worst hand that you would ordinarily draw to. If you wouldn't draw to less than a pair of sevens in a particular situation, use the row in Table 4.3b that has a pair of sevens as its leftmost entry. This row says that your best bluffing hand should be 88AKQ when the pot contains 1 bet, 88KQJ when the pot contains 2 bets, and 88QJ10 when the pot contains 3 bets.

TABLE 4.3a
Maximum Bluffing Hands for the Opener*

Worst Hand He Opens With	Bets in Pot		
	1	2	3
KK	KK8	KK8	KK7
QQ	QQ10	QQ10	QQ9
JJ	JJQ	JJQ	JJ10
99	99A	99K	99A
66	779	779	66A
22	33K	33K	33K

* The hands listed represent the highest acceptable bluffing hands. In other words, an entry of KK8 means that one should bluff with KK876 or worse. Note that the requirements in Tables 4.3a and 4.3b are not affected in any obvious way by the size of the pot. The reason for this is given in the text.

TABLE 4.3b
Maximum Bluffing Hands for the Second Player to Speak

Worst Hand He Might Have Drawn To	Bets in Pot		
	1	2	3
AA	AA9	AA9	AA8
KK	KKJ	KK9	KK8
QQ	QQJ	QQ10	QQJ
1010	1010A	1010A	1010A
77	88A	88K	88Q
44	66A	66J	55A

Observant readers may notice that the size of the pot has no obvious effect in either Table 4.3a or 4.3b. This is because the size of the pot actually has two effects that tend to cancel each other out. A large pot implies that a player should bet more, but it also implies that he should bluff less often per bet. For example, when the pot contains 1 bet, a player who opens with kings or better should bet with aces up or better (Table 4.2a) and bluff once for every 2 times he bets legitimately.* When the pot contains 2 bets, he should bet more (with any two pairs), but he should bluff less per bet (only once for every 3 legitimate bets). It turns out that he should bluff with the same number of hands in both cases.

PROBLEM

There is $30 in the pot. Your opponent now bets $10. How frequently should you call to make sure that he breaks even in the long run by bluffing?

Answer: He is risking $10 to win $30, so you should call or raise 3 times for every time that you drop. (You should call or raise three-fourths, or 75%, of the time.)

Problem: When the pot contains 2 bets, Table 4.2a indicates that a player who opens with jacks or better should bet whenever he improves, which will happen 29% of the time (Table 4.1). What percentage of *time* should he bluff?

Answer: After he bets, there will be 3 bets in the pot, so his opponent will be getting 3 to 1 odds. Therefore, he should bluff 1 time for every 3 times that he bets legitimately. Since he only bets legitimately 29% of the time, or approximately 3 times in 10, this means he should bluff 1 time in 10. In other words, in the 7 times out of 10 that he doesn't improve, he should bluff once.

Expected Gain from Bluffing Correctly

Your gain by bluffing correctly will depend almost entirely on how badly your opponents play. To get a feel for what kinds of gains are possible, suppose your single opponent calls only when he improves, as one book recommends. Let's assume that the pot contains $40 and the limit

---

* If there is 1 bet in the pot before he bets, there will be 2 bets in the pot afterwards, so his opponent will be getting 2 to 1 odds. Therefore, he must bluff 1 time for every 2 times that he bets legitimately. If there were 2 bets in the pot initially, he would have to bluff 1 time for every 3 times that he bets legitimately.

is $20. If your hand is hopeless, you will gain $40 by bluffing whenever your opponent drops, which should happen 71% of the time (Table 4.1). You will lose $20 by bluffing whenever he calls or raises, which should happen 29% of the time. Your expected gain by bluffing in this situation is therefore (.71) × $40 − (.29) × $20 = $22.60. In other words, every time you bluff against this player you will gain a wopping $22.60! If your game had $4 in the pot and the limit was $2, you would gain $2.26.

It should be noted at this point that most players do not call as badly as the example might suggest. However, even if your opponent called 50% of the time in the above example, you would still make $10 per bluff.

CALLING STRATEGY

When your opponent bluffs too much, call with any hand that can beat a bluff. This might mean calling with kings if your opponent opens with jacks or better. If he bluffs too little, drop unless you can beat some of his legitimate hands. If he never bets legitimately with less than queens up, drop with less than kings up.

Whether your opponent overbluffs or underbluffs can be determined with some difficulty by comparing his bluffing habits to the correct bluffing strategy. He should bluff in such a fashion that your pot odds equal the odds against his bet being a bluff. In other words, if the pot is offering you 2 to 1 odds after he bets, he should bluff once for every two legitimate bets. If he only bluffs once for every four legitimate bets, he is bluffing too little. This means that you should drop unless you can beat some of his legitimate hands.

When you don't know how your opponent plays, use Tables 4.4a and 4.4b. If you follow these tables, you will be calling the correct percentage of time, and the hands you will be calling (raising) with will be your best ones. It is useful to note that the requirements in Tables 4.4a and 4.4b decrease as the odds offered by the pot increase. This means that you have to call more when the pot is large.

TABLE 4.4a
Minimum Calling Hands for the Opener

Worst Hand He Opens With	Bets in Pot*		
	2	3	4
KK**	KK66	AAJ	AA10
QQ	AAK	AA10	AA9
JJ	AA9	KKQ	KKJ
99	KKJ	QQ10	QQ4
66	QQK	JJ4	99A
22	JJ4	88J	77A

* In this case "bets in pot" refers to the number of bets that are in the pot *after* your opponent has bet. It doesn't make any difference here whether your opponent has bet the limit or not.

** The entries in this row assume that your opponent was marked with aces before the draw. This assumption allows you to drop whenever you have kings. You should call more if your opponent may have drawn to less than aces.

TABLE 4.4b
Minimum Calling Hands for the Second Player to Speak

Worst Hand He Might Have Drawn To	Bets in Pot		
	2	3	4
AA	AAK	AAJ	AA10
KK	AAJ	AA4	KKQ
QQ	AA4	KKQ	KK4
1010	KKQ	QQK	JJA
77	QQK	JJ4	99A
44	JJA	99K	77A

PROBLEM

You put the opener on jacks or better since you're playing Jackpots. He typically bets when he's improved, and he calls with kings or aces after checking. He checks. There are three final-round bets in the pot. What do you do with (a) AAJ84; (b) QQ852?

Answer: Table 4.2a indicates that he's betting okay, but Table 4.4a indicates that he's calling too much (he should only call with some kings, not with all of them). Consequently, it won't pay to bluff. You gain by betting with aces against a player who calls correctly (Table 4.2b), so you will also gain by betting against someone who calls too much. Therefore you should bet with the first hand and check with the second.

RAISING STRATEGY

The basic idea behind raising strategy is that a raising hand should win most of the time *when your opponent calls.* It doesn't help to raise and have him drop. The raising strategy presented here was determined by figuring out how often your opponent *should* call (or raise) and then making sure that you would win at least 55% of the time when that happened.

When using Table 4.5, it is useful to remember that the table was computed by assuming that the opener approximately follows Table 4.2a. If he doesn't, it may be advan-

TABLE 4.5
Minimum Raising Hands for the Second Player to Speak

Worst Hand He Might Have Drawn To	Bets in Pot*			
	1**	2	3	4
AA	AAA	AAA	AAA	AAA
KK	AAA	AAA	KKK	KKK
QQ	AAA	KKK	KKK	KKK
10 10	KKK	KKK	QQQ	QQQ
77	KKK	QQQ	10 10 10	10 10 10
44	QQQ	JJJ	888	888

* In this case "bets in pot" refers to the number of bets that are in the pot after your opponent has bet.

** This column gives the requirements for pot limit. The "1" signifies the fact that your raise equals the pot.

tageous to modify your strategy somewhat. For example, suppose you wouldn't draw to less than tens in this situation, which presumably means that your opponent's minimum opening hand is somewhere around sevens. If the pot contained 2 bets when it was his turn to bet, Table 4.2a indicates that he should be betting with sevens and deuces or better.* If he actually bets with a minimum of jacks up, he figures to have a somewhat better hand than Table 4.5 anticipated, so you should increase your raising requirements from three queens (row 1010, column 3) to three kings.

CONTESTS INVOLVING A ONE-CARD DRAW

When you draw one card, your opponents should never be sure that you have two pairs or three of a kind. If they always are certain that you have such hands when you draw one, they will not call you after the draw with less than a medium two pairs. In this case you can often take advantage of them by drawing one card to a pair and then betting as though you actually have two pairs.

For example, suppose you open with your minimum of jacks and get called by one player. Presumably he has you beat, but he probably has less than two pairs since he didn't raise. If he puts you on two pairs in these situations whenever you draw one, then he should drop unless he makes at least two pairs. This means that he should drop roughly 70% of the time (Table 4.1), so you will profit greatly by bluffing. If you do not bluff against this player, you will be passing up a golden opportunity.

To protect himself in these situations, your opponent should call a certain percentage of time, given by Rule 9.4 of Chapter 9. He can use Table 4.4b to determine what hands to call with whenever he drew to a pair. For example, suppose he normally draws to a minimum of kings in this situation. (He knows that you open with a minimum of jacks.) If there are 3 bets in the pot when it is his turn to act, he should call with a minimum of aces (Table 4.4b, row KK, column 3).

---

* The assumption is that he started with at least sevens.

When your opponent calls in this fashion, you can use Table 4.2a to determine what hands will be profitable to bet. In the present case, your minimum betting hand should be threes up. Suppose now that you open and get raised. In this case you must consider the possibility that your opponent is bluffing. If he is, it will usually be to your advantage to check after the draw.

Many players who raise before the draw also bet afterwards, so there is often little point in betting yourself. However, if you do decide to bet, you should be able to beat your opponent at least 60% of the time when he calls (or raises). Since he won't always call, it is approximately equivalent to say that you should be able to beat him at least two thirds of the time whether he calls or not. If you put him on threes up or better, this means you need at least three fours (Table 3.9). If you put him on nines up or better, you need at least three eights.

THREE-PLAYER CONTESTS

Understandably, three-player contests are considerably harder to analyze than two-player contests. Therefore, this section will give some general rules for guiding your decisions, and then present some problems which are meant to illustrate the ways three-player contests may be analyzed. The problems are hard and are meant for advanced players. However, reading the problems and the answers should be quite valuable.

General Rules

Let's label the players in the order that they must speak, i.e., player 1 will speak first, then player 2, then player 3.

1. Players 1 and 3 need stronger hands to bet than they would if they were alone in the pot. This is simply because player 2 is an additional threat. For positional reasons, player 2 needs a stronger hand than player 3, but can bet with a weaker hand than player 1.

As an example, suppose that each player drew three
cards, and that there are two bets in the pot. Let's say
the opener, player 1, figures to have nines or better,
and that his opponents have better than nines. Ordinarily against one opponent, player 1 could bet with
threes up (Table 4.2a). However, in this case, because
of the additional threat from player 2, he needs at
least aces up. Player 2 needs a little less, around kings
up. Player 3 should probably have at least queens up,
because his opponents are unlikely to call with pairs.

2. Players 2 and 3 need better hands to raise than they
   would in a two-player contest. For example, instead of
   three queens they might need three kings. This is
   primarily because player 1 figures to be betting better
   hands.

3. When player 1 bets, player 2 should call only if he can
   beat some hands that player 1 would bet legitimately.
   This also goes for player 3 if player 1 checks and player
   2 bets, etc.

   To illustrate, suppose that player 1 bets. If player 3
   wasn't in the pot, player 2 would have to call part of
   the time with a pair (Table 4.4b). At present, player 2
   shouldn't call with less than aces up. Let player 3 worry
   about the possibility that player 1 is bluffing.

4. If player 1 bets and player 2 drops, player 3 should
   call (raise) player 1 almost as often as he would if player
   2 wasn't in the pot. This is because player 2 won't be
   calling very much, so player 3 will have most of the
   burden of discouraging a bluff. The same sort of statement can be made for player 1 if player 2 bets and
   player 3 drops, etc.

5. Each player should bluff the same number of times per
   legitimate bet as he would against one opponent (Rule
   9.6).

PROBLEMS FOR ADVANCED PLAYERS ————————

The following problems may require the use of Rules
9.4 and 9.7 of Chapter 9. We have already discussed both of
these rules. Rule 9.7 says that a bettable hand should be

able to win at least 60% of the time when it is called or raised. Rule 9.4 says that your opponents should call and raise in such a fashion that the odds against your winning by bluffing equal your pot odds.

Problem: You open in a position where you would ordinarily open with jacks or better and two players call, each drawing three. They figure to have higher pairs than jacks since they know how you play. You make aces up, and the pot contains three final-round bets. What do you do?

Answer: Your opponents should call or raise roughly 3 times for every time that they drop (Rule 9.4) because they can't afford to let you make money bluffing them out with jacks or queens. Equivalently, they should call or raise 3 times out of 4, or 75% of the time. You only figure to lose 24% of the time (Table 4.1). Therefore, using Rule 9.7, you should bet.

Problem: Take the previous problem except that you opened in seventh seat with aces. Is the correct play obvious, and if so, what is it?

Answer: In this case your opponents apparently called with medium pairs* and they probably know that you had them beat. Therefore they aren't going to call with less than two pairs.** In fact, the player to your left probably won't call with less than three of a kind. As a result, most calls will be made by three of a kind or better, so you will lose by betting.

If you check with the intention of calling, you will also lose. The player to your left probably won't bet with less than three of a kind, and the last player may or may not bet with two pairs. In other words, most of your calls will lose. The correct play is therefore not clear-cut. If your opponents like to bluff, a check is probably superior. If they tend to call whenever they improve, a bet will probably be less damaging.

* This might happen when your opponents are the Ante and Straddle.
** This is not a contradiction of Rule 9.4. To understand why, look at the precise formulation of that rule on page 192.

Problem: Your pass and out game has a total ante of 1 bet. The player in third position opens, someone else calls, and you call with kings. The limit is doubled after the draw so that the pot contains two final-round bets. The opener and first caller check to you. They both drew three initially. You suspect that either player would have bet with three of a kind or better. What do you do with kings up?

Answer: Both players are presently marked with two pairs or less. Since you figure to get called by and beat most two pairs, you should bet.

Problem: You open and draw three while two opponents who called draw one. Neither player figures to be drawing to a flush or straight since their pot odds were insufficient. After the draw there are two bets in the pot. You make kings up. What do you do?

Answer: Both players are almost certainly marked with less than kings up since neither raised. The implication is that you will win unless one of them makes a full house, which won't happen over 18% of the time (entry 5, Table 3.11). You figure to be called or raised roughly 2 times out of 3 (Rule 9.4), because your opponents can't afford to let you make money bluffing with a single pair. Therefore, using Rule 9.7, you should bet.

5

WINNING STRATEGIES FOR LOWBALL: THE FIRST ROUND

Lowball, which in England is called Misère, has become quite popular in recent years. In California it is probably played more than any other game. This popularity is partially due to the fact that Stud Poker is not legal in California, so that Lowball and other draw games have a monopoly in the legal clubs. Whatever the reason for its popularity, it is a game that deserves considerable attention because there are players who have beaten the game for hundreds of thousands of dollars.

Lowball is played just like Draw, except that the order of the hands is reversed, i.e., one wishes to make as low a hand as possible. Consequently, although a pat eight — 85432 — is a sure loser in Draw, it becomes a very good hand in Lowball.

At present there is no uniform way of ranking Lowball hands. Most clubs consider an ace to be low,* but there is a split over straights and flushes. Some clubs consider straights and flushes to be high, others do not. I will assume that straights and flushes may be counted as low hands, and that an ace is low. Therefore, 5432A, or a "wheel," is the best possible hand. Any adjustments in strategy that should be

---

* An ace is considered as a "1." In other words, the ranking of the individual cards is K, Q, J, 10, 9, 8, 7, 6, 5, 4, 3, 2, A.

made when other rules are in effect will be discussed at the
end of the chapter.

Lowball is usually played with a "bug," or joker, included
in the deck. The strategies presented here assume that the
bug is included, although it generally makes little difference. The most significant effect of the bug is to make the
very fine hands easier to get. For example, a wheel is about
twice as easy to get with the bug in the deck. However, the
probability of being dealt a pat nine, for example, is only
changed from 2.76% to 3.00% when the bug is included.

As you read this chapter, remember that the term "bet"
will always refer to a limit-size bet, and that the tables in
this chapter are meant for flat limit. Playing requirements
for pot limit should in general be stricter. Also, pat hands
lose some of their value in pot limit because they tend to do
poorly after the draw.

Readers interested in learning how some of the tables in
this chapter were computed should read Chapter 9 and the
Appendix.

A SAMPLE DEAL OF LOWBALL

For those not familiar with Lowball, it may be helpful to
go through a sample deal. The cards dealt to each of eight
players are shown below.

Pam	K7752
Arch	Q9876
Joan	9542A
John	KJ843
Caroline	QQQ22
Lucky	K10986
Lois	9643A
Richard	K843A

Since the average winning hand in Lowball is somewhere
around a good nine, e.g., 96543, Pam shouldn't bet unless
she has a pat hand like 97652 or 8742A, or a hand like

K8542 or 7742A, which has a good chance of developing into at least an eight after the draw. Pam has two bad cards, so she drops. (I'm assuming the rules are pass and out.) Arch has a chance of making a rough (poor) nine, but this hand may not win even if he makes it, so he drops also. Joan has a smooth (good) nine, which is a good hand, so she bets the limit, which we will assume equals the total ante. John, Caroline, and Lucky drop. Lois raises the limit. It now costs Richard 2 bets to call. He must draw a card, and he has no guarantee of winning even if he makes an eight. Consequently, he drops. Joan calls. Joan must draw first and can either rap pat or *break* (draw). She decides to draw and throws away her nine. Lois raps pat. Joan catches a five, giving her 5542A. At this point Joan has no chance of winning if she checks, since a pair of fives is a very bad hand at Lowball. She decides to bluff. Alas, Lois calls and wins the pot.

OPENING REQUIREMENTS FOR PASS AND OUT GAMES

Opening requirements will vary from game to game, but they should follow some logical pattern. One author has claimed that the minimum opening requirements in a bad position (positions 6 or 7) should be a pat 97654 and a one-card draw to 8654. This implies that 98654 should be opened because it contains 8654, but that it shouldn't be opened because it is worse than 97654. Such advice is illogical.*

The following table presents a good opening strategy for an ordinary pass and out game with a total ante of 1 bet. A discussion of how the table was computed is given in Section 2 of the Appendix.

To see how the table may be used, suppose your game has a total ante of $20 and a limit of $20, or a total ante of $10

---

* It is unlikely that the author meant that one should open with 98654 and then draw one card. That play is almost always wrong.

and a limit of $10, or a total ante of $2 and a limit of $2. In all these cases the total ante equals 1 bet, so the table is applicable. Against three opponents your minimum opening hands should be 109876 and 972A. Against one opponent you only need J10987 or 94A. Opening with 94A may seem a bit loose, but it is important to realize that your opponent's median hand will be around 72A. The final-round betting* and the consistency** of the deck were taken into account in computing the table.

TABLE 5.1a

Opening Requirements for an Ordinary Pass and Out Game with a Total Ante of One Bet*

Players Yet to Speak	Minimum Pat Hand	Minimum Drawing Hand
7	98765	8543
6	98765	864A
5	98765	8732
4	109876	943A
3	109876	972A or 432
2	J10987	742
1	J10987	94A

*The requirements in this table should be tightened slightly, say from 8543 to 7654, if your opponents call and raise with weaker hands than they should. (The correct calling and raising strategies will be given later.) This table should not be used for Ante and Straddle games (see Table 5.1b).

The requirements listed in Table 5.1a assume that the bug is not in the hand. If you hold the bug, you can reduce the requirements slightly. For example, you can open with 874 Bug in seventh position and with 54 Bug in fourth position.

* The opener was assumed to have the worst position after the draw.

** A passed hand has, on the average, approximately one eighth of a low card less than an average hand of five cards. Consequently, when a number of players pass, the remaining players are likely to have slightly more low cards than usual, and hence slightly better hands.

It should be noted that Table 5.1a need not be memorized unless it applies to your game. Also, when it does apply, it need not be memorized exactly. There is no harm in using a strategy close to Table 5.1a but easier to remember. For example, a good opening strategy would be to open with a minimum of 8543 in position seven, 8543 in position six, 8654 in position five, 9432 in position four, 9654 in position three, 654 in position two, and 876 in position one. This strategy is almost as accurate as that given in Table 5.1a, and it is much easier to remember. One way of remembering it would be as follows: 85, 85, 86, 94, 96, 6, 8.

ADJUSTMENTS FOR OTHER GAMES

Lowball is generally played with a total ante of around 1 bet, but it is generally not played with an equal ante from all players. In other words, some players may ante more than others. After one complete deal, however, each player ends up having anted the same amount.

"Unequal ante" games may be classified as being either Ante and Straddle or Big Blind. For either type of game it may be necessary to make minor adjustments in Table 5.1a.

Ante and Straddle Games

Most games around San Francisco are of this form. Typically, the player in first position (called the Ante) puts in one chip, and the player in zeroth position (the Straddle) puts in two chips. The player in second position (the dealer) puts in a chip as well. These four chips constitute the total ante, which typically equals 1 bet.

The contributions of the Ante, Straddle, and dealer are considered to be part of any bet, call, or raise they may decide to make. This rule has the effect of reducing the amount of money that the opener stands to win whenever he is called or raised by the Ante, Straddle, or dealer. As a result, the opener stands to win less on the average by opening in an Ante and Straddle game, so he needs a better hand to do so.

The following table presents a good opening strategy for games in which the Ante and dealer put in one chip and the Straddle puts in two chips. The entries should be tightened (from 98765, 7654 to 98543, 762A, etc.) if opponents call and raise with weaker hands than they should.

TABLE 5.1b
Opening Requirements for an Ante and Straddle Game with a Total Ante of One Bet

Players Yet to Speak	Minimum Pat Hand	Minimum Drawing Hand
7	98765	7654
6	98765	8432
5	98765	863A
4	109876	874A
3	109876	9432
2	J10987	987A or 54A
1	J10987	76A

Big Blind Games

"Big Blind" games are common in Gardena, California. In a $10 limit Big Blind game, everyone puts in a dollar, and one player, called the *Blind,* puts in a blind bet of $10. Thus there is typically $18 in the total ante. The player who opens generally does so by raising the Blind $10. The opener puts $20 into a pot containing $18, so the total ante is approximately one "bet." In order to open in the average game, one must have at least 7654 or 98765 in the seventh position, and at least 987A or 54A in first position. After the pot is opened, players may raise at most $10.

Games in Which the Limit Is Doubled After the Draw

The opening requirements I have given in Tables 5.1a and 5.1b are meant for games in which the limit equals the total ante both before and after the draw. The requirements should be tightened slightly when the limit is doubled after the draw, because this has the effect of making the game somewhat more like pot limit.

CALLING STRATEGY BEFORE THE DRAW

Against One Opponent

As was the case in draw poker, the quality of the opener's hand is the single most important calling consideration. However, the position of the caller is also important. When the caller has bad position, he needs a better hand than he would ordinarily because of the threat from players behind him.

Table 5.2 illustrates these points. Notice that the requirements in any column go down as the opener's hands weaken. Similarly, the requirements in any row go down as your position improves.

Table 5.2 was designed for an ordinary pass and out game, but it may also be used for Ante and Straddle or Big Blind games. The entries should be tightened slightly in a Big Blind game (from 874A to 852A, etc.) and the Blind should use Table 5.3 when he is getting 4 to 1 odds. In an Ante and Straddle game the requirements in positions 4 and 3 should be tightened (from 765A to 753A, etc.) because the Ante, Straddle, and dealer can call and raise for less. Antes and Straddles should use Table 5.3 rather than Table 5.2.

To see how Table 5.2 may be used, suppose that the total ante is $5 and that someone bet $4. Let's say this player figures to have anywhere from 98765 on down if he has a pat hand, and his worst one-card draw figures to be somewhere between 8654 and 7654. You are in third position. In this case you should use the column with the "3" at the top. If the total ante were 1 bet, your minimum calling hand would be somewhere between 8642 (the entry in your column directly across from the "98765 or 8654") and 853A (the entry in your column directly across from the "98765 or 7654"). Since the total ante is slightly over 1 bet, you can afford to call with the 8642.

TABLE 5.2
Minimum Calling Hands Against One Opponent
When the Total Ante Equals One Bet*

Opener's Worst Hand**	Your Position				
	4	3	2	1	0
97654 or 7543	7543	7643	842A	854A	8642
98765 or 7654	765A	853A	8642	874A	8765
98765 or 8654	8432	8642	8743	943A	9642
109876 or 972A	864A	8763	965A	982A	9876

Calls may also be made with rough nines and in some cases with rough tens.

*Entries should be tightened somewhat in Ante and Straddle and in Big Blind games.

** A 97654 and 7543 are typical minimums for a tight player in sixth or seventh position.

A 98765 and 7654 are typical minimums for a good player in sixth or seventh position in an Ante and Straddle game.

A 98765 and 8654 are typical minimums for a good player in fourth position in an Ante and Straddle or Big Blind game, and in fifth position in an ordinary pass and out game.

A 109876 and 972A are typical minimums for a good player in second position in an Ante and Straddle or Big Blind game, and in third position in an ordinary pass and out game.

When you know nothing about the opener, assume that he plays well. For example, suppose the opener is in third position and you are in second position. The game is an ordinary pass and out. In this case Table 5.1a indicates that his worst opening hands should be slightly worse than 109876 or 972A, since the total ante is slightly over 1 bet. Using Table 5.2, we see that your worst calling hand should therefore be slightly worse than 965A. (The correct minimum turns out to be around 9754.)

Readers who do not wish to memorize all of Table 5.2 may find it convenient to remember just the correct strategies for first and third positions and then use those to guide their play in other positions. It is also useful to note that the entries in Table 5.2 need not be memorized exactly.

PROBLEM ———————————————————————————————————

You hold 762A in sixth position in an Ante and Straddle game with a total ante of 1 bet. A complete stranger in seventh position opens. What do you do?

Answer: Assuming he plays well, the opener should have a minimum of around 98765 or 7654 (Table 5.1b). With this assumption, Table 5.2 indicates that 765A represents a minimum call from fourth position in an ordinary game. You have a slightly better hand but your position is worse. Furthermore, the Ante and Straddle can call cheaply. The correct play is therefore to drop.

Calling Strategy for the Ante and Straddle

In Ante and Straddle games the Ante and Straddle will typically be getting either 3 to 1 or 4 to 1 odds to call the opener. Consequently they can afford to call with weaker hands than usual; notably, with two- and sometimes even three-card draws. Table 5.3 gives the minimum acceptable standards for calling in these situations. The table assumes that (a) the opener is alone in the pot and (b) the caller is last to speak. When the caller has active players behind him, he should increase his requirements. If he has a two-card draw and there are two or more players in the pot, he

TABLE 5.3
Minimum Calling Hands for the Ante and Straddle*

Opener's Worst Hand	Odds Offered by Pot	
	3 to 1	4 to 1
97654 or 7543	875A	54A
98765 or 7654	965A	654
98765 or 8654	64A	85A
109876 or 972A	854	98A

* Entries assume that the Ante speaks first after the draw. This is generally the case in Ante and Straddle games.

should generally drop. This is because his chances will be cut considerably by the presence of more players while his pot odds will be only slightly improved.*

Calling Against More Than One Opponent

As you may recall, in Draw Poker the second player to call needs a slightly better hand than the first player, and this is true in Lowball as well. Entries 9 and 25 of Table 5.11 serve to support this claim. In entry 25, 8642 has a 45% chance against a smoother one-card draw. However, in entry 9 it only has a 24.8% chance against two smoother one-card draws. In other words, a hand that does well against one player may not do so well against two or more players. Therefore a player who calls against two or more players needs a better hand.

RAISING STRATEGY

Raising strategy before the draw in Lowball is complicated by the fact that a raise may persuade a pat hand to break and draw. Consequently, many seemingly "automatic" raises are actually wrong. For example, suppose you have 87654 and your opponent has 96543. Let's say you opened, he raised, and now it's your turn. If you reraise he's certain to break, and hence have a good chance of winning. However, if you flat call and rap pat, he may rap pat too, in which case you have a certain win. This example suggests some interesting practical questions. Suppose for the sake of discussion that you open with a minimum of 98765 or 8654. Then we can ask:

1. What hands should an opponent raise you with?
2. What hands should you reraise with?
3. What hands should you break if he raises?
4. What hands should he break if you call his raise and rap pat?
5. What hands should he break if you reraise?

* A detailed explanation is given after Table 5.11.

Before reading the answers to these questions, try and answer them yourself, say for the special case when the opener's worst hands are 98765 and 8654. It turns out that the analysis is quite complicated, because all of the answers are tied together. In other words, how often the opener reraises affects how often his opponent should raise, etc.

The answer to the first question is partially dependent on the size of the ante and on the raiser's position. In a good position the main concern should be whether to call or raise. In this respect 9864A will be borderline regardless of the size of the ante. In a bad position it may be best not to play at all. A 9864A should be dropped in fifth or sixth position when the total ante is 1 bet. The probability is too great that someone behind you will call (or raise) with a better hand. However, if the total ante were 2 bets, the larger ante would make raising with 9864A profitable in all positions.

Table 5.4 gives good raising and reraising strategies for games with a total ante of 1 bet. The table may be used in a fashion similar to Tables 3.6a and 3.6b. For example, the raiser should be guided by the opener's minimum hand. If the opener figures to have a minimum of 98765 or 7654, then the raiser needs at least 97654 (second row,

TABLE 5.4
Raising and Reraising Strategy When
the Total Ante Equals One Bet*

Opener's Minimum Hand	Minimum Raising Hand	Minimum Hand Opener Should Reraise With
97654 or 7543	97543	7652A
98765 or 7654	97654	7654A
98765 or 8654	9864A**	8542A
109876 or 972A	98765 or 6543	87542

* The entries will also be quite good for games with somewhat larger antes.

** This requirement should be replaced by 97654 in positions five and six.

Table 5.4). When the raiser is not familiar with the opener, he should assume that the opener plays well. If the opener is in third position in an ordinary game, then his minimum hand *should* be around 109876 or 972A (Table 5.1a). Therefore the raiser needs at least 98765 or 6543 (fourth row, Table 5.4).

The opener's correct reraising strategy may be determined in a similar fashion. If the raiser figures to have at least 97543, then the opener needs at least 7652A to reraise (first row, Table 5.4). When the opener is not familiar with the raiser, he should assume that the raiser plays well. If the opener's minimums are 98765 and 8654, then he should assume that the raiser's minimum is 9864A (third row, Table 5.4), which means that the opener needs at least 8542A to reraise.

Raising Against More Than One Opponent

In general, raising requirements with pat hands should be increased slightly when several players call the opener, whereas raising requirements with one-card draws should be decreased slightly. In other words, if A opens and B calls, C will need a slightly better pat hand to raise than he would if B wasn't in the pot. However, he can raise with a somewhat weaker one-card draw. For example, instead of raising with a minimum of 98765 or 6543, he might raise with a minimum of 97654 or 7543.

The fact that smooth one-card draws do better than rough nines in large contests is well illustrated by entry 2 of Table 5.11. Observe that 9864A has a 29.1% chance in a typical contest with three other players, whereas 643A has a 33.1% chance. In other words, a smooth draw does better in contests with a large number of players. Hence it also represents a better raising hand.

BREAKING STRATEGY

To illustrate some of the ideas behind breaking strategy, consider a situation in which the opener calls the raiser and raps pat. Presumably the opener likes his hand since he did not break. Therefore, if the raiser has one of his worst raising hands, he may be tempted to break. But should he? If his drawing chances are greater than his chances of having the best hand, then he should break, otherwise he should not. To make a good decision, the raiser needs to know his chances of winning if he draws, as well as the worst hand that the opener would rap pat with. If the raiser is off by as little as 10%, his error will cost over $5 in a $10-limit game.

Tables 5.5a and 5.5b give the correct breaking strategies for both the opener and the raiser. They may be used in the same fashion as Table 5.4. For example, if the raiser's minimum is 97654, then the opener should break all hands between 9432A and 98542 when he gets raised (second row, Table 5.5a). He should drop with worse hands unless the total ante is large (2 bets) or his opponent is prone to bluffing.

The raiser's best breaking hand should depend on the best breaking hand of his opponent. If the opener breaks with 97432 or worse, then the raiser should break with 9543A or worse when the opener calls and raps pat (third row, Table 5.5b). As usual, if either player is not familiar

TABLE 5.5a
Breaking Strategy for the Opener

Opener's Minimum Hand	Raiser's Minimum Hand	Breaking Hands for the Opener
97654 or 7543	97543	9432A through 97654
98765 or 7654	97654	9432A* through 98542**
98765 or 8654	9864A	97432 through 98654**
109876 or 972A	98765 or 6543	10432A through 109765***

* The 9432A appears in both the first and second rows because there is a big gap between a smooth nine and a rough eight. A smooth nine can improve a lot when broken, whereas a rough eight can only improve a little. Consequently, it pays to break a smooth nine but it does not pay to break a rough eight.

** Pat hands that are worse than the ones listed should be dropped when the total ante is 1 bet or less. They should generally be broken when the total ante is greater than 1 bet.

*** Draw one card when you break. Rap pat with 1098xx if your opponent has a tendency to raise as a bluff or if the total ante is greater than 1 bet. Drop otherwise.

with his opponent, he should assume that his opponent plays well.

When the opener gets raised he should generally drop with his roughest pat hands as I have indicated. However, against some opponents he may do better if he calls and then raps pat as a bluff. For example, consider a situation in which you open with 98765 and your opponent raises, presumably with at least 9864A. If you rap pat, he will assume that you have a fairly good pat hand since you did

TABLE 5.5b
Breaking Strategy for the Raiser
After the Opener Calls and Raps Pat*

Raiser's Minimum Hand	Best Hand That the Opener Breaks	Best Hand That the Raiser Should Break
97543	9432A	87543
97654	9432A	87543
9864A	97432	9543A
98765 or 6543	10432A	97654

* Entries were computed assuming that the opener does not rap pat with his worst hands as a bluff. If he does, slightly fewer hands should be broken.

not break or drop. As a result, he may break a fair number of pat hands out of fear. If he breaks hands better than 96432, you will gain by calling and then rapping pat.

Breaking After a Reraise

Suppose that someone opens, you raise, and the player who opened reraises. In this case you will generally have to make a choice between two unpleasant alternatives. If your opponent typically reraises with 7652A or better, then you will certainly want to break (or drop) with anything worse than 7652A. In fact, you may want to break somewhat better hands as well. The problem is that if you do this, you will end up breaking (or dropping) with about

80% of your raising hands whenever you get reraised. Once your opponent notices this, he will start to reraise with bad hands just to get you to break (or drop). As a result you will have different best strategies depending on how your opponent plays. If he always reraises with strength, then you should break (or drop) with most of your hands. However, if he reraises more than one third of the time as a "bluff," then you should almost never break (or drop).

This situation is analogous to bluffing situations after the draw. If a player never bluffs, his opponents should never call with a mediocre hand (in this case, rap pat with a mediocre hand). However, if he bluffs a lot, they should almost always call.

TABLE 5.6
Breaking After a Reraise

Opener's Worst Hand	Opener's Worst Legitimate Reraising Hand	Best Hand That Should Be Broken Against an Expert*	Best Hand That Should Be Broken Against a Player Who Doesn't Bluff*
97654 or 7543	7652A	87432	7643A
98765 or 7654	7654A	87542	7653A
98765 or 8654	8542A	87643	8432A
109876 or 972A	87542	97632	8732A

* See preceding discussion for explanation.

Table 5.6 presents two sets of strategies for this situation. The right column gives the best strategy against players who always reraise with strength. For example, if your opponent reraises with 8542A or better, then you should break (or drop) with 8432A and anything worse (third row, Table 5.6).

The second column from the right gives a strategy that should be used against players capable of a bluff. If hands better than those listed in this column are played pat, an expert will not be able to gain by reraising with rough nines. If fewer hands are played pat, he will.

CALLING AFTER A RAISE

Once the opener is raised, a player who has not yet spoken must decide whether he wants to put in 2 bets to play. In many games it is routine for players to pay 2 bets to draw to a smooth seven. As you can see from the fourth row of Table 5.7, such a play is often correct when the opener may be weak. For example, if the opener may have as bad as 109876 or 972A (approximately), then 7543 represents a minimum call. However, paying 2 bets to draw to a seven can also be an extremely bad play, as evidenced by the requirement of 87432 in the first row.

TABLE 5.7
Minimum Requirements for Entering a Raised Pot When the Total Ante Is One Bet*

Opener's Minimum Hand	Raiser's Minimum Hand	Minimum Calling Hand
97654 or 7543	97543	87432
98765 or 7654	97654	87542
98765 or 8654	9864A	96432** or 6432
109876 or 972A	98765 or 6543	97543*** or 7543

* The requirements in this table may be loosened slightly in a Big Blind game because the caller is only putting in 1½ times the size of the opening bet.
** Rap pat with 87654 or better.
*** Rap pat with 97543 or better if the raiser draws. Otherwise, rap pat with 9652A or better.

In an expert game, a player who is known to raise with no worse than 97654 may have to break his hand if someone comes in to call for 2 bets. Presumably the caller will have 87542 or better (second row, Table 5.7), so the raiser would have almost no chance of winning if he rapped pat with, say, 95432.*

The situation changes somewhat if the raiser is known to raise with all nines. In this case the caller might have a smooth draw (fourth row of Table 5.7) and the raiser's best play with 98765 would be to rap pat.

CALLING AFTER BEING RAISED

The correct strategy for calling after you open and are raised is given in Table 5.5a. This table essentially says that you should call with everything except possibly some of your roughest pat hands. For example, the third row of the table says that you should drop with worse than 98654 when your opponent raises with a minimum of 9864A. This means that you can call with 8654 (your worst one-card draw) since you should call with 98654 and then break.

SNOW JOBS

The term "snow job" refers to any type of first-round bluff in Lowball. Most players who "snow" end up raising and reraising until everyone drops out or they get called. To give an example of the potential of such a play, I was sitting in a twenty limit one night when I opened with 7432. The betting then went call, raise, call, and it was back to me. I called. My left-hand opponent, who had initially called with 97532, now decided to raise, hoping somehow to get his opponents to break their hands and draw. He was in turn reraised, and then the action subsided, with everyone except the reraiser drawing one card. After the draw the man who had done most of the raising bet again and everyone folded. He collected the pot of $340.

The moral of the story is that the reraiser may have had a full house for all we know, and still be snickering to him-

---

* His only chance would be that the caller might break. This chance is usually too small to warrant rapping pat.

self. He simply kept betting until everyone threw his hand away.

In general, the best situation to "snow" is when you are in first or zeroth position, and there is only one person already in the pot. You simply raise, rap pat, and then bet after the draw, as though you had a seven. If your lone opponent happened to draw two cards, you are a heavy favorite to bluff him out. In general, you should stop making this play for a while after you are caught.

EFFECT OF THE FINAL ROUND

Because Lowball is a game of fine percentages, the final round becomes rather important, and it must be taken into account when a decision to bet, call, or raise is made. In particular, it is important to know how much a positional advantage is worth, and how a pat hand will do after the draw. This of course will vary with the caliber of play, but one can get a good idea by assuming that everyone plays well. The figures below are based on this assumption.

Constant Limit Games

In games with a constant limit in both rounds, an opener with an average one-card draw figures to lose on the last round because he must speak first. Against a single one-card draw, this loss will usually be about .09 of a bet. It will be less against two or more players. The opener will generally gain against a pat hand that raised. When the opener has a rough pat nine, he figures to lose approximately .24 of a bet. This is because he must call a significant portion of the time to protect against a bluff and he cannot bet.

Pot Limit Games

In pot limit games the losses for the one-card draw and the pat hand become, respectively, .17 and .42 of a first-round bet.* The larger losses are attributable to the larger bets

---

* I assume that bets on both rounds equal the pot.

that may be made on the final round. Because of these losses, opening requirements should be tightened somewhat in pot limit.

MATHEMATICAL TABLES

This section contains some tables used to compute most of the strategies presented in this chapter and the next. The first two tables are listings of pat hands and one-card draws. Each of the hands listed in a particular table is just as likely to be dealt as any other when there is no bug in the deck. When the bug is included, its primary effect will be to slightly increase the probability of being dealt a smooth hand.

The numbers that appear to the left of certain hands are meant to be used for determining how many hands are higher or lower than a specific hand. For example, 49 hands fall below 8764A, and $126 - 50 = 76$ hands are above it. Consequently, if you have 8764A and your opponent has any pat hand 98765 or better, the odds of your having the better hand are about 76 to 49 in your favor.

Table 5.10 gives the probability that a specific hand will be "better" than any hand held by various numbers of opponents. For example, the entry of 53% in the second row from the top and under the 3 says that among three opponents, the best hand figures to be, on the average, a one-card draw to a rough eight. Consequently, if you have a chance to open from third position with 8765, you know that your hand is probably as good as anything your remaining three opponents might have. This information would indicate that you should open unless the total ante is very small (less than half a bet).

The first eight rows in Table 5.10 give *cumulative* information, i.e., the chances that various numbers of opponents hold *at least* a certain hand. The last eight rows give *specific* information, i.e., the chances that the best hand among three players will be *specifically* a pat nine. Entries in the table change only slightly if straights and flushes are counted or

TABLE 5.8
List of Pat Hands

126	98765		97654		87654		76543
	98764	90	97653	55	87653	20	76542
	98763		97652		87652		7654A
	98762		9765A		8765A		76532
	9876A		97643		87643		7653A
	98754		97642		87642		7652A
120	98753	85	9764A	50	8764A	15	76432
	98752		97632		87632		7643A
	9875A		9763A		8763A		7642A
	98743		9762A		8762A		7632A
	98742		97543		87543		75432
115	9874A	80	97542	45	87542	10	7543A
	98732		9754A		8754A		7542A
	9873A		97532		87532		7532A
	9872A		9753A		8753A		7432A
	98654		9752A		8752A		
110	98653	75	97432	40	87432		65432
	98652		9743A		8743A	5	6543A
	9865A		9742A		8742A		6542A
	98643		9732A		8732A		6532A
	98642		96543		86543		6432A
105	9864A	70	96542	35	86542		
	98632		9654A		8654A		5432A
	9863A		96532		86532		
	9862A		9653A		8653A		
	98543		9652A		8652A		
100	98542	65	96432	30	86432		
	9854A		9643A		8643A		
	98532		9642A		8642A		
	9853A		9632A		8632A		
	9852A		95432		85432		
95	98432	60	9543A	25	8543A		
	9843A		9542A		8542A		
	9842A		9532A		8532A		
	9832A		9432A		8432A		

TABLE 5.9
List of One-Card Draws

70	8765	35	7654	15	6543	5	5432
	8764		7653		6542		543A
	8763		7652		654A		542A
	8762		765A		6532		532A
	876A		7643		653A		432A
65	8754	30	7642	10	652A		
	8753		764A		6432		
	8752		7632		643A		
	875A		763A		642A		
	8743		762A		632A		
60	8742	25	7543				
	874A		7542				
	8732		754A				
	873A		7532				
	872A		753A				
55	8654	20	752A				
	8653		7432				
	8652		743A				
	865A		742A				
	8643		732A				
50	8642						
	864A						
	8632						
	863A						
	862A						
45	8543						
	8542						
	854A						
	8532						
	853A						
40	852A						
	8432						
	843A						
	842A						
	832A						

if the bug is removed. In these cases the percentages for one,
two, and three opponents will normally be off by less than
2%.

Some important observations may be made from Table
5.10:

1. The probability of a particular player holding a pat nine
   or better is extremely small, about $\frac{1}{18}$.
2. The probability of any of seven opponents holding a pat
   nine or better is about $\frac{1}{3}$; for a 97654 or better, it is
   about $\frac{1}{4}$; and for an eight or better, it is about $\frac{1}{6}$.
3. If a player always raps pat with a nine or better, the odds
   favor him having a nine when he raps pat.
4. The average best hand held between two players is
   9765; between three, 8752; between four, 8543; and
   between five, 765A.*
5. If a player normally opens with a minimum of 98765
   or 7654, the odds are 17 to 11 that he will draw if he
   opens.

Table 5.11 gives the chances of winning in most of the
situations encountered before the draw. For example, if you
have a smooth two-card draw and your opponent has a
smooth one-card draw, then entry 29 gives you about a
35% chance of winning in a showdown.

The entries in Table 5.11 were computed by assuming
that the only cards taken out of the deck were either in the
hands listed or in the rightmost column of the table. For
example, in entry 19 the only cards taken out of the deck
were assumed to be 8, 7, 5, 3, 2, 7, 4, 3, A, and K. In practice, the cards taken out of the deck will also include all
the cards in passed hands. Because a passed hand figures to
have about $\frac{1}{8}$ of a low card less than an average hand of five
cards,** the preceding assumption slightly underestimates
the number of low cards in the remainder of the deck. The

---

* I assume that a pat nine is better than 765A. This assumption has a minimal
effect.
** This was determined by using a computer.

TABLE 5.10
Distribution of Hands

Number of Players

	1	2	3	4	5	6	7
Probability that at least one of them holds a pat nine or better or a							
9876 or better	34%	57%	72%	82%	88%	92%	95%
8765 or better	22%	39%	53%	63%	71%	77%	82%
7654 or better	14%	26%	36%	45%	53%	60%	66%
6543 or better	9½%	18%	26%	33%	39%	45%	50%
Probability that at least one of them holds a pat							
9 or better	5½%	11%	16%	21%	25%	29%	33%
8 or better	2½%	5%	7½%	10%	12½%	14½%	16½%
7 or better	1%	2%	3%	4%	5%	6%	7%
6 or better			1%			2%	
Probability that the best hand held* is a one-card draw to a							
9	12%	18%	19%	19%	17%	15%	13%
8	8%	13%	17%	18%	18%	17%	16%
7	4½%	8%	10%	12%	14%	15%	16%
6 or 5	4%	7%	10%	12%	14%	16%	17%
Probability that the best hand held is a pat							
9	3%	6%	8½%	11%	12½%	14½%	16½%
8	1½%	3%	4½%	6%	7½%	8½%	9½%
7, 6, or 5	1%	2%	3%	4%	5%	6%	7%

*These entries assume that a pat nine is better than any one-card draw. This assumption only slightly affects the entries (by 1 or 2%).

TABLE 5.11
Probability of Winning in a Variety of Contests
(Figures given below assume there is no bug in the deck)

Entry	Hand 1	Hand 2	Hand 3	Hand 4	Other Cards Originally in the Hands
1	86532	7642	852A	63A	KKJ3
	65.3%*	14.6%	12.7%	7.4%	
2	9864A	643A	7542	732	KQQ J
	29.1%	33.1%	28.1%	9.7%	
3	632A	7642	54A**	732	KKQQ JJ
	44.1%	31.6%	9.6%	14.7%	
4	86532	852A	63A		KKQ
	70.5%	21.0%	8.5%		
5	9764A	543A	7542		KQ
	36.4%	34.2%	29.4%		
6	9652A	643A	7543		KQ
	41.8%	35.0%	23.2%		
7	9764A	7542	73A		KKQ
	47.0%	38.3%	14.7%		
8	9764A	53A***	742		KQQ J
	69.3%	15.0%	15.7%		
9	653A	743A	8642		KQJ
	39.8%	35.4%	24.8%		
10	653A	743A	642		KKQJ
	42.8%	40.5%	16.7%		
11	843A	642	73A		KQQJJ
	51.1%	23.1%	25.8%		
12	109642	653A	743A		KQ
	27.6%	37.7%	34.7%		

* Probability of winning in a showdown.

** This figure is lower than that for the 732 because there are only 7 cards seven or under left in the deck that don't pair the A45, while there are 9 cards that don't pair the 732.

*** Similar reasoning.

TABLE 5.11 (Continued)

Entry	Hand 1	Hand 2	Hand 3	Hand 4	Other Cards Originally in the Hands
13	9642	653A	743A		KQJ
	21.1%	41.9%	37.0%		
14	10653A	743A	642		QQJ
	45.3%	39.6%	15.1%		
15	7642A	7532			K°754∧
	86.0%	14.0%			
16	8642A	7532			K9753A
	78.0%	22.0%			
17	8754A	7532			K9763A
	70.0%	30.0%			
18	97532	743A			K
	59.5%	40.5%			
19	87532	743A			K
	69.0%	31.0%			
20	7653A	643A			K
	78.5%	21.5%			
21	432A	9764			KQ
	62.9%	37.1%			
22	432A	8764			KQ
	59.9%	40.1%			
23	432A	7654			KQ
	57.9%	42.1%			
24	432A	6543			KQ
	57.0%	43.0%			
25	7542	8642			KQ
	55.0%	45.0%			
26	753A	974A			KQ
	59.3%	40.7%			
27	643A	743A			KQ
	53.4%	46.6%			

TABLE 5.11 (Continued)

Entry	Hand 1	Hand 2	Hand 3	Hand 4	Other Cards Originally in the Hands
28	8642 70.6%	875 29.4%			K Q J
29	753A 64.9%	742 35.1%			K Q J
30	8642 58.8%	52A 41.2%			K Q J
31	9752 56.0%	74A 44.0%			K Q J
32	74A 54.5%	2A 45.5%			K Q J 42
33	8642 64.8%	2A 35.2%			K Q J A
34	32A 58.1%	876 41.9%			K Q J 10

consequence of this is that a one-card draw's chances versus a pat hand are underestimated in the table by between 1 and 3%. However, when all players are drawing, the error due to this assumption should be negligible.

We may conclude from Table 5.11 that a two-card draw will do worse when the number of players in the pot increases. To see this, suppose that the total ante equals 1 bet. In entry 2, a typical four-player contest, the 732 figures to get back 5 (bets) × 9.7% (chance of winning) = .49 of a bet for the bet it puts in: a loss of .51 of a bet.* In entry 7, a typical three-player contest, it figures to lose .41 of a bet. In entry 29, a typical two-player contest, it figures to *gain* .05 of a bet.

---

* I am neglecting the final-round betting for the sake of simplicity.

Notice how dramatically the two-card draw is affected by the entry of a third player into the pot. Always drop a two-card draw against two other players unless you are getting pot odds of at least 6 to 1.

Table 5.12 gives the probability of making various hands by drawing either one or two cards. Observant readers may notice that there is a jump of 7% between the probabilities of making a six and a seven (bug included), whereas there is a jump of 9% between the probabilities of making an eight and a nine. This is because the other players' cards were taken into account. Players in the pot are more likely to have sevens than nines, so the probability of making exactly a seven is less than that of making exactly a nine.

TABLE 5.12

Probability of a Player Making Various Hands by Drawing Either One or Two Cards*

		Drawing One Card		Drawing Two Cards	
			Bug in Deck		Bug in Deck
Probability of	88	100%	100%		
Making at	77	97½%	97½%	92½%	93%
Least	66	94½%	95%	88%	89%
	55	92%	93%	83½%	85%
	44	89½%	90½%	79%	81%
	33	87%	88%	74½%	77%
	22	84%	86%	70%	73%
	AA	81½%	83½%	65½%	69%
	K	79%	81%	61%	65%
	Q	69%	71%	50%	54%
	J	59%	61%	38%	41%
	10	50%	52%	29%	32%
	9	40%	42%	20%	22%
	8	31%	33%	14%	16%
	7	23%	25%	8%	9%
	6	16%	18%	4%	5%

* The entries assume that the bug is not in the player's hand.

The entries for making, say, an eight or better in Table 5.12 are only valid if the player is drawing to a hand that contains no nines, etc. The percentages for pairs assume that the player on the average draws to 8765 or better, or, in the case of two-card draws, to 765 or better. Of course, if your opponent is drawing to 643A, then he can't make a pair of sevens, but *on the average* he will make a pair of sevens about 3% of the time when he draws one card.

TABLE 5.13
Probability of Winning Against an Opponent Who Rapped Pat

Entry	Your Hand	Opponent's Hand	Probability of Your Winning in a Showdown
1	8765	98765 or better	17%
2	8765	97654 or better	8%
3	8654	98765 or better	23%
4	8654	97654 or better	18%
5	8654	87654 or better	10%
6	8543	98765 or better	26%
7	8543	97654 or better	20%
8	8543	87654 or better	14%
9	7654	98765 or better	28%
10	7654	97654 or better	22%
11	7654	87654 or better	16%
12	7654	76543 or better	2%
13	7543	98765 or better	31%
14	7543	97654 or better	26%
15	7543	87654 or better	21%
16	7543	76543 or better	9%
17	6543	98765 or better	33%
18	6543	97654 or better	30%
19	6543	87654 or better	24%
20	6543	76543 or better	14%
21	5432	98765 or better	35%
22	5432	97654 or better	33%
23	5432	87654 or better	27%
24	5432	76543 or better	19%

If your hand contains the bug, use the next highest entry (bug not in deck) to compute your chances. For example, if you have 85ABug, your chances of making an eight or better are approximately equal to your chances under ordinary conditions of making a nine or better, i.e., about 40%.

The figures for making a six or better in Table 5.12 are somewhat misleading because they assume that your opponent is drawing to 6543 or better (654 or better for the two-card draw). In actual play your opponent may not be able to make a six since he may have started with something like 7642. Tables 6.17a, b, c, and d in Chapter 6 can be used to get the probability that he will make a six or better when you have some idea of the worst hand that he may have drawn to.

Table 5.13 gives your chances of beating an opponent who rapped pat. For example, if you suspect that your opponent may have anywhere from 98765 on down, and you have 7543, then your chances of winning are about 31% (entry 13).

DRAWING PROBLEMS

Most Lowball hands are rather straightforward to draw to, but questions occasionally come up. The following problems are meant to be solved by using an appropriate combination of Tables 5.11, 5.12, and possibly 5.13.

PROBLEM ————————————————————————

You are playing in a game where the limit is fairly small in relation to the ante. An opponent opens, another calls, and you call with 10963A. Each opponent takes one card. What do you do?

Answer: Entry 12 of Table 5.11 gives you about a 27.6% chance of winning by rapping pat. If you draw one card to 963A, entry 13 gives you about a 21.0% chance. If you draw two cards, entry 10 lists your chances as slightly better than 16.7%. (The one-card draws against you don't figure to be quite as good as those in entry 10.) It is unlikely that you will make a hand that is bettable by drawing either one or two cards, and since the limit is also low you should definitely rap pat.

PROBLEM

You hold 9863A and have every reason to believe that your opponent has at least 97654. Do you draw one card or two?

Answer: Table 5.13 gives you about a 20% chance if you draw one. If you draw two, you will probably need at least an eight to win. Your chances of making such a hand are about 16% (Table 5.12). Therefore you should draw one.

ADJUSTMENTS FOR THE SIX-FOUR AND SEVEN-FIVE SCALES

The preceding strategies have been based on what is known as the California scale. In the California scale, 5432A is the best hand. Other scales currently in use are often referred to as the six-four and seven-five scales. In the six-four scale, straights and flushes are considered to be high. Therefore 6432A is the best hand. In the seven-five scale, aces as well as straights and flushes are counted for high. Therefore 75432 is the best hand.

To go from the six-four scale to the seven-five scale, simply increase each card a notch. For example, 8543A in the six-four scale becomes 96542 in the seven-five scale. Similarly, 6432A in the six-four scale becomes 75432 in the seven-five scale.

A good approximate rule for going from the California scale to the six-four scale is to relax each requirement by "five hands" on the first round and by "three hands" on the second round. In other words, if the minimum first-round raising hand on the California scale is 97654, then the minimum first-round raising hand on the six-four scale should be 9852A (see Table 5.8). Similarly, if the minimum opening hand on the California scale is 863A, then the minimum opening hand on the six-four scale should be 865A. After the draw, only the betting and raising requirements need be adjusted.* A minimum raising hand of 76432 should become 76532.

The above rule was formulated by comparing the California scale to the six-four scale for both pat hands and one-card draws. In the six-four pat hand scale, 5432A, 65432, 76543, 87654, and 98765 are gone, along with all low flushes (which are rare). If we count all the low flushes as one hand, then 97654 is about five hands better when viewed on the six-four scale. Similarly, 76432 is about three hands better.

In the six-four one-card draw scale, 5432 and ♣6♣3♣2 ♣A are worse than 9432, and 7632 is about the same as 432A. Using this information, the following hands would probably be ranked as being worse than 863A on the six-four scale: 7654, 7653, 7643, 7543, 6543, 5432. Neglecting low four flushes (which are rare), we see that 863A is about six hands better when viewed on the six-four scale. Therefore we should relax 863A by about six hands to find its equivalent on the six-four scale.

* The calling strategy doesn't have to be changed because it doesn't make much difference whether your minimum calling hand is Q8532 or Q8543 (see Table 6.3).

6

WINNING STRATEGIES FOR LOWBALL: THE SECOND ROUND

This chapter presents the second half of a winning system for Lowball. The tables that will be given are applicable to both pot limit and flat limit games. I will explain how the tables should be used as they are presented.

The tables give strategies for anywhere from three to five different values of pot odds so as to cover games with different antes and limits. If you only play in one game, you will probably only need to know the correct strategies for one value of pot odds. This means that you only need to remember a small fraction of each table (usually two entries). After you memorize a couple of entries from a couple of tables, you should already have an edge.

When learning the tables, do not place much importance on remembering strategies exactly. If the correct strategy is to bet with 87642 or better, and you remember to bet with any eight or better, you will be close enough.

BETTING RULES

At present there are no uniform rules concerning betting after the draw. Three rules are in common use, however:

1. You must bet a seven or better (this is known as the sevens rule)
2. No checking and raising
3. Anything goes

In practice, Rules 1 and 2 are about the same. The sevens rule requires you to bet a seven, six, or five if you have one. You don't have to bet these hands when Rule 2 is in effect, but it turns out that it is almost always right for you to do so. Consequently, from a practical point of view, the two rules are about the same.

The strategies given in this chapter were computed assuming that Rule 2 was in effect. If your game follows Rule 1, then you should use the strategies without adjustment unless they tell you to check a rough seven. In this case you must bet.

When your game follows Rule 3, you should also use the strategies without adjustment except that it may be right for you to occasionally check with a good hand like a six. You will have to decide this for yourself.

ONE-CARD DRAW VERSUS ONE-CARD DRAW

This section presents the correct strategies for a two-player contest in which each player has drawn one card. Other types of contests will be considered in subsequent sections.

BETTING STRATEGY

For the First Player to Speak

We have already observed that a good betting strategy should be affected by the size of the pot. When the pot is large, your opponent will have to call more (with weaker hands) to prevent you from making money by bluffing. Consequently, you can afford to bet weaker hands. The

correct strategy is also slightly affected by the hand your
opponent drew to. If his hand was smooth, he figures to
make smooth hands, so you should have a slightly better
hand than usual to bet.

The leftmost column of Table 6.1a takes into account the
strength of your opponent's hand. If he made a routine
call in a good position, he may have had anywhere from
8765 on down, and the first set of entries should be used.
However, if he raised he probably had at least 742A, so
the last set of entries would be more appropriate.

As a simple example of the use of Table 6.1a, suppose

TABLE 6.1a
Betting Strategy for the
First Player to Speak

Worst Hand Opponent Might Have Drawn To	Bets in Pot	Minimum Betting Hand
8765	1	8542A
	2	87432
	3	87642
	4	87654
	5	9754A
8642	1	7653A
	2	8643A
	3	87532
	4	87654
	5	9732A
7654	1	7632A
	2	76542
	3	87432
	4	87654
	5	9653A
742A	1	65432
	2	76532
	3	86432
	4	87654
	5	95432

that your game has a total ante of $10, and a limit of $10 before and after the draw. You open and one opponent calls. At this point there will be $30, or 3 final-round bets, in the pot. If your opponent figures to have drawn to anywhere from 8765 on down, then you should use the first set of entries. The correct entry to use in this set is the one across from the "3" in the "bets in pot" column. This is 87642. If your opponent had instead drawn to at least 742A, then you would use the last set of entries. The correct entry to use would again be the one across from the "3" in the "bets in pot" column. This is 86432.

My purpose in presenting four different tables is simply to indicate how the strategies change as the hands your opponent may have been drawing to improve. As you can see, the entries don't change very much. Furthermore, the worst hand an opponent may have drawn to will typically be around 8765, and it will rarely be as good as 742A. Consequently, the rest of the tables will be given for only one "worst draw." A player who draws one card will be assumed to have at worst 8765. Also, a player who raps pat will be assumed to have at worst 98765. I will always indicate when these assumptions may have a significant effect on the strategies being presented.

The hands listed in Table 6.1a were determined by the condition that the average gain from betting against an expert be equal to the average gain from checking. If your opponent calls less than he should, your average gain by betting will go down and you should probably check with borderline hands. I will discuss how to spot such players in the section on bluffing.

Betting Strategy for the Second Player to Speak

Since the first player shows weakness by checking, the second player can bet with weaker hands. As an illustration, Table 6.1b indicates that the second player can bet with 10875A when the pot contains 3 bets. This hand was determined by the condition that it win half the time when the first player calls, assuming that the first player calls correctly. If the first player calls too little, the betting requirements should be tightened slightly. For example, the first player should call with K642A or better when the pot contains 4 bets* (Table 6.3). If he only calls with a jack or better, the minimum betting hand for the second player should be 107642.

TABLE 6.1b
Betting Strategy for the
Second Player to Speak

Bets in Pot	Minimum Betting Hands
1	8765A
2	98765
3	10875A
4	J754A
5	J862A

BLUFFING STRATEGY

The ideas behind bluffing strategy were discussed in Chapter 4. When you are unfamiliar with your opponent, use Table 6.2.

TABLE 6.2
Bluffing Strategy

Bets in Pot	Bluffing Hands for	
	First Player to Speak*	Second Player to Speak
1	6632A or worse	22853 or worse
2	55864 or worse	3342A or worse
3	55864 or worse	33865 or worse
4	66543 or worse	4476A or worse
5	6685A or worse	5532A or worse

*Observant readers may notice that the size of the pot has no obvious effect on the first player's strategy. The reason for this is similar to that given on page 69.

*There will be 4 bets in the pot after the second player has bet.

If your opponent calls too much, bluff as little as possible without being obvious. If he calls too little, bluff with any hopeless hand. In Lowball, a hopeless hand is a pair of fours or worse. Table 6.3 will often be helpful in determining whether your opponent "overcalls" or "undercalls." For example, suppose you face a player who never calls with worse than a jack. If the pot will contain 4 bets after you have bet, Table 6.3 indicates that he should call with some kings; he's not calling enough. This means that you should bluff with a pair of fours or worse.

CALLING STRATEGY

Calling strategy for Lowball is similar to calling strategy for Draw. The best strategy against a player who bluffs too much is to call with any hand that can beat a bluff. This might mean calling with threes if necessary.

The best strategy against a player who bluffs too little is to drop unless you have a chance of beating some of his legitimate hands. If he only bets with eights or better, this means that you should drop with worse than an eight.

Whether your opponent overbluffs or underbluffs can often be determined by comparing his bluffing habits to the strategies given in Table 6.2. For example, Table 6.2 indicates that the first player to speak should never bluff

TABLE 6.3
Calling Strategy

| Bets in Pot* | Minimum Calling Hands for | |
	First Player to Speak	Second Player to Speak
2	10864A	10872A
3	Q642A	Q8532
4	K642A	K7632
5	K8532	K8752
6	KQJ109	2287A

*Includes your opponent's bet.

with better than fives. If you see someone bluff with a pair of deuces or threes, you can presume that he bluffs too much.

When you are not familiar with your opponent, use Table 6.3. An explanation of the logic behind this table, as well as behind bluffing and calling tables in general, is given in Chapter 9.

PROBLEM ————————————————————————————————

A popular book has claimed that (a) one will be a big winner in the long run by bluffing with two fives if the pot contains 5 bets, but (b) a loser if the pot contains 3 bets, and (c) one will be a big loser in the long run by bluffing against two or more players unless his pot odds are enormous. Why are all these statements incorrect?

Answer: The first statement presumes that the player's opponents will sit back and let him make money at their expense. If they called correctly, he would break even by bluffing with fives.

The last two statements imply that his opponents are calling too much and are thereby losing money unnecessarily when he bets legitimately. This condition can be remedied as well.

RAISING STRATEGY

As indicated in Chapter 4, a raising hand should be able to beat its competition at least 55% of the time when it is called (or raised). The entries in Table 6.4 were determined by figuring out how often your opponent should call, and then making sure that you would win at least 55% of the time when that happened.

Bear in mind that Table 6.4 and the other raising tables assume that your game has a flat limit. If your game has a pot limit and you are raising the pot, tighten the entries.

Table 6.4 may be used in the same fashion as the other tables. If the pot contained 2 bets at the beginning of the round, your worst raising hand should be 75432 (second row, Table 6.4). If the pot contained 3 bets at the beginning of the round, your worst raising hand should be 76432 (third row, Table 6.4). The "bettor's worst hand" column is included simply to show you what your opponent should be betting with. If he deviates considerably from the correct strategy, you should adjust your strategy to take advantage of his error. For example, when the pot contains 2 bets, he *should* bet with a minimum of 87432 (second row). If you know that he never bets with less than 85432, you can tighten your strategy. In this case your worst raising hand should be 7432A.

TABLE 6.4
Raising Strategy

Bets in Pot at the Beginning of the Round	Bettor's Worst Hand	Minimum Hands for	
		Raising	Reraising
1	8542A	65432	6432A
2	87432	75432	6542A
3	87642	76432	65432
4	87654	7653A	7432A
5	9754A	7654A	7532A

Unfortunately, the correct raising strategy is noticeably affected by the worst hands that each player may have drawn to. The strategies given in Table 6.4 were computed assuming that both players drew to anywhere from 8765 on down. If either player figures to be drawing considerably smoother, the requirements should be tightened. For example, if both players drew to anywhere from 7654 on down and the sevens rule is in effect, the worst raising hands for 1, 2, 3, 4, and 5 bets in the pot should be 6543A, 65432, 7532A, 7543A, and 75432 respectively.

ONE-CARD DRAW VERSUS TWO-CARD DRAW

One-Card Draw Speaks First

These contests differ from contests involving two one-card draws because a two-card draw is a weak hand. Consequently, a one-card draw can bet more against a two-card

draw than it would against another one-card draw. Tables
6.5 through 6.8 cover situations in which the one-card draw
speaks first. They may be used in the same fashion as Tables
6.1a, 6.1b, 6.2, 6.3, and 6.4.

It is useful to observe from the tables that the two-card
draw can bet with relatively bad hands. This is because the
one-card draw shows considerable weakness by checking.
The two-card draw's bluffing requirements are rather high
because it makes so many bad hands. Notice that the one-
card draw should bluff more against a two-card draw than
it would against another one-card draw. This is because it
bets more, so it must also bluff more to keep the same ratio
of bets to bluffs.*

STRATEGY FOR A CONTEST INVOLVING
A ONE-CARD DRAW AND A TWO-CARD DRAW
(The One-Card Draw Speaks First)

TABLE 6.5
Minimum Betting Hands

Bets in Pot	One-Card Draw	Two-Card Draw
1	87642	10642A
2	9765A	J643A
3	98765	J875A

TABLE 6.6
Bluffing Hands

Bets in Pot	One-Card Draw	Two-Card Draw
1	2287A or worse	66Q2A or worse
2	4432A or worse	66K2A or worse
3	4485A or worse	7765A or worse

* Rule 9.6 of Chapter 9.

TABLE 6.7
Minimum Calling Hands

Bets in Pot*	One-Card Draw	Two-Card Draw
2	J852A	J765A
3	Q875A	Q864A
4	K864A	K8432

*Includes your opponent's bet.

TABLE 6.8
Minimum Raising Hands

Bets in Pot at the Beginning of the Round	Minimum Betting Hand for the One-Card Draw	Minimum Raising Hand for the Two-Card Draw	Minimum Reraising Hand for the One-Card Draw
1	87642	7543A	6532A
2	9765A	7652A	6542A
3	98765	76542	6543A

Two-Card Draw Speaks First

In many games a two-card draw rarely speaks first because that would mean that it opened the pot. However, in Ante and Straddle games, the Ante has to speak first after the draw, and he is one of the few players who bets or calls with a two-card draw. Consequently, I am rather accustomed to seeing a two-card draw speak first.

In these situations the two-card draw rarely bets because it rarely makes a hand worth betting. For example, it only figures to make a seven or better 9% of the time (Table 5.12). From the one-card draw's point of view, the situation after the two-card draw checks is rather similar to a situation in which the one-card draw actually had to bet first. True, the one-card draw can bet with slightly weaker hands because there is no danger of a raise, but in general Tables 6.5 and 6.6 should provide fairly good betting and bluffing strategies. Similarly, Table 6.7 yields a good calling strategy for the two-card draw. The correct calling strategy for the one-card draw is given in the right-hand column of Table 6.3.

PAT HAND VERSUS ONE-CARD DRAW

Contests involving pat hands can get complicated by the fact that the pat hand may be nothing more than a "snow job," e.g., 2222A. However, most players don't snow; and if they do, they tend to snow from some positions but not from others, so it is usually possible to rule out a snow in most cases.

Pat Hand Speaks First

The first group of tables assumes that the pat hand speaks first and is not snowing. The entries were computed assuming that the pat hand could be anything from 98765 on down, and that the one-card draw could be anything from 8765 on down.

When the sevens rule is not in effect, the correct strategy for the pat hand is to always check, which wipes out most of the entries. Consequently, a set of tables is included to give the correct strategy when the sevens rule is in effect. This set indicates that the pat hand should bluff with its very worst nines, so as to motivate the one-card draw to call with eights. If the pat hand doesn't bluff occasionally, the one-card draw will have no reason to call with worse than a seven. The pat hand must bluff if it wants to make money on its good hands.

Table 6.10 indicates that the pat hand should bluff with 98765, 98764, 98763, and 98762 when the pot contains 4 bets. If you never play such hands in a particular situation and follow the table, you will end up never bluffing. To avoid this problem, you should always bluff with your four worst hands. If you open with a minimum of 97654, you should bluff with 97654, 97653, 97652, and 9765A.

A somewhat similar problem comes up as far as calling is concerned. The correct strategy for the pat hand when there are 4 bets in the pot and the sevens rule is in effect is to call with a minimum of 9854A (Table 6.11). The 9854A was computed by assuming that the worst hand you play pat is 98765. If you never play with worse than 97654 in a certain situation, you won't have any hands to drop with if you follow the table. In this situation your worst calling hands when there are 2, 3, 4, and 5 bets in the pot should be 87654, 96532, 9743A, and 9753A, respectively. Readers interested in learning how to compute strategies for themselves should read Chapter 9 and the Appendix.

Betting and raising requirements are slightly affected by the strength of the pat hand. If the pat hand figures to be 97654 or better, these requirements should be tightened somewhat. Specifically, when the pot contains 1, 2, 3, and 4 bets and the sevens rule is in effect, the worst betting hands for the one-card draw should be 8742A, 8754A, 8762A, and 87632, respectively.

STRATEGY FOR A CONTEST INVOLVING
A PAT HAND AND A ONE-CARD DRAW
(The Pat Hand Speaks First)

TABLE 6.9
Minimum Betting Hands
When the Sevens Rule Is Not in Effect

Bets in Pot	Pat Hand	One-Card Draw
1	— *	8652A
2	—	8752A
3	—	8763A
4	—	8764A

* The correct strategy is always to check.

Minimum Betting Hands
When the Sevens Rule Is in Effect

Bets in Pot	Pat Hand	One-Card Draw
1	76543	8762A
2	76543	87653
3	76543	9543A
4	76543	9642A

TABLE 6.10
Bluffing Hands
When the Sevens Rule Is Not in Effect

Bets in Pot	Pat Hand	One-Card Draw
1	—	55743 or worse
2	—	55864 or worse
3	—	6632A or worse
4	—	6632A or worse

When the Sevens Rule Is in Effect

Bets in Pot	Pat Hand	One-Card Draw
1	98742 or worse	33765 or worse
2	98753 or worse	4476A or worse
3	9876A or worse	55743 or worse
4	98762 or worse	55864 or worse

TABLE 6.11
Minimum Calling Hands
When the Sevens Rule Is Not in Effect

Bets in Pot*	Pat Hand	One-Card Draw
2	9642A	—
3	97632	—
4	9842A	—
5	98542	—

* Includes your opponent's bet.

When the Sevens Rule Is in Effect

Bets in Pot*	Pat Hand	One-Card Draw
2	9742A	8732A
3	97653	87632
4	9854A	8765A
5	9864A	9643A

* Includes your opponent's bet.

TABLE 6.12
Minimum Raising Hands When the Sevens Rule Is in Effect

Bets in Pot at the Beginning of the Round	Betting Requirements for the Pat Hand	Raising Requirements for the One-Card Draw	Reraising Requirements for the Pat Hand
1	76543	6543A	6432A
2	76543	65432	6432A
3	76543	65432	6432A
4	76543	7432A	6532A

One-Card Draw Speaks First

Generally, when the one-card draw speaks first, it opened and was then raised by the pat hand. The tables below make this assumption. When the pat hand flat calls, it shows weakness (often a ten) and the situation is completely different. This latter possibility is covered in the problems.

Tables 6.13 through 6.16 were computed by assuming that the first player to speak had anywhere from 8765 on down before the draw, and that his opponent had anywhere from 98765 on down. The second player's bluffing strategy should be adjusted as indicated in the last section if his minimum raising hand is not 98765. If he typically raises with 97654 or better, his worst calling hands for 2, 3, 4, 5, and 6 bets in the pot should be 87542, 9543A, 9653A, 9732A, and 97432, respectively. In this case the betting and raising requirements for both players should be tightened slightly.

STRATEGY FOR A CONTEST INVOLVING A PAT HAND AND A ONE-CARD DRAW
(The One-Card Draw Speaks First)

TABLE 6.13
Minimum Betting Hands

Bets in Pot	One-Card Draw	Pat Hand
1	85432	8742A
2	8654A	87542
3	87542	87642
4	87632	9632A
5	8765A	9753A

TABLE 6.14
Bluffing Hands

Bets in Pot	One-Card Draw	Pat Hand
1	55864 or worse	98643 or worse
2	66754 or worse	98653 or worse
3	66754 or worse	9873A or worse
4	66852 or worse	9873A or worse
5	7732A or worse	9873A or worse

TABLE 6.15
Minimum Calling Hands

Bets in Pot*	One-Card Draw	Pat Hand
2	87632	9642A
3	87653	97632
4	9753A	9843A
5	98432	98542
6	98542	9864A

* Includes your opponent's bet.

TABLE 6.16
Minimum Raising Hands

Bets in Pot at the Beginning of the Round	Minimum Betting Hand for the One-Card Draw	Raising Requirements for the Pat Hand	Reraising Requirements for the One-Card Draw
1	85432	65432	6432A
2	8654A	7543A	6542A
3	87542	7643A	65432
4	87632	7652A	7432A
5	8765A	76532	7532A

THREE-PLAYER CONTESTS

The same general rules that were given in Chapter 4 for three-player contests apply to Lowball contests as well. Betting and raising requirements should be somewhat more strict in three-player contests than they were in two-player contests. The first player to speak needs a better hand to bet than the second, who in turn needs a better hand than the third. A player who is threatened by someone behind him should call only if he has a chance of beating a legitimate bet. The last player to speak, however, should call almost as often as he would ordinarily.

These rules are well illustrated by the following analysis of a three-player contest. It is instructive to compare the strategies given below to strategies that have been given for two-player contests.

ANALYSIS OF A THREE-PLAYER CONTEST IN WHICH EACH PLAYER DRAWS ONE CARD

Let's agree to call the three players 1, 2, and 3, and have player 1 speak first, etc. The sevens rule is in effect. I assumed that each player's worst possible draw was 7654. If the draws in your game could have been rougher, you should reduce the requirements slightly. You should also reduce the betting, bluffing, and raising requirements if one or more opponents draw two cards. However, the calling requirements in this case should remain about the same.

The following strategies are meant for situations in which the pot contains 3 bets, but they may also be used to approximate good strategies when the pot contains either 2 or 4 bets.

Decisions for Player 1

Player 1 should bet with 76543 or better. If he checks, player 2 bets, and player 3 folds, he should call with Q7542 or better. When player 2 checks and player 3 bets, player 1 needs 97643 or better to call. Player 1 should bluff with 6653A or worse.

Decisions for Player 2

If player 1 checks, player 2 should bet with 8763A or better. If player 1 bets, player 2 should call with a minimum of 7652A. When he checks, player 3 bets, and player 1 passes, player 2 needs K542A or better to call. He needs 87643 or better to call after player 3 has bet and player 1 has called. He should bluff with 55742 or worse.

Decisions for Player 3

When his two opponents check, player 3 should bet with 10542A or better. If player 1 bets and player 2 passes, he needs at least Q754A to call. If player 1 bets and player 2 calls, he needs a minimum of 7643A to overcall. If player 1 passes and player 2 bets, he needs at least 8743A to call. He should bluff with 5563A or worse.

PROBLEMS FOR ADVANCED PLAYERS ──────────

Problem: You draw two cards, and your opponent draws one card and bets. He generally bluffs with a pair of sixes or worse, and he roughly follows Table 6.5 as far as betting is concerned. There are three bets in the pot. You hold J762A. What do you do?

Answer: Table 6.6 indicates that he's not bluffing enough. Consequently you should fold any hand that cannot beat a legitimate bet, i.e., you should fold.

Problem: In a game that follows the sevens rule, you rap pat with 98765 and your opponent draws one. He typically calls with any eight in these situations. There are 2 bets in the pot and you speak first. What do you do?

Answer: Your opponent is calling too much (Table 6.11). Therefore it won't pay to bluff with this hand.

Problem: You opened and your opponent merely called with a pat hand. He routinely raises with a nine in these situations. There are 2 bets in the pot, and you make 98764. What do you do?

Answer: Your opponent probably would have raised with 98765 or better, so you have an almost certain winner. Therefore you should bet.

Problem: You open with a one-card draw, and your opponent, who occasionally snows in these situations, raises. You make 8742A. There are 3 bets in the pot. What do you do?

Answer: Table 6.13 indicates that your worst betting hand should be 87542, i.e., you may make a little by betting. However, if your opponent was snowing, you will do much better by checking. Therefore you should check.

Problem: A opens, you call, and B calls. A raps pat, you draw one, and so does B. A figures to have started with 97654 or better; B probably had at least 7654. The sevens rule is in effect, but A checks. There are 4 bets in the pot. What do you do with 85432?

Answer: Table 6.1a indicates that 87654 should be your worst betting hand when A isn't in the pot. Since A's check indicates that you are almost certain to have him beat, you can afford to bet.

DISTRIBUTION OF MADE HANDS

The following tables were used to compute many of the strategies given in this chapter. As an example of their use, suppose that your opponent drew to 8765 or better and made an eight or better. (You might know that he made an eight or better because his worst betting hand is 87654 and he just bet.) In this case, Table 6.17a indicates that 7632A figures to beat him all but 20% of the time (sixth entry from the bottom). This means that you should probably raise if you hold such a hand (Rule 9.8).

If your opponent had instead drawn to 8642 or better, you would have a 28% chance of losing (Table 6.17b) and your decision might be a little closer.

TABLE 6.17a
Distribution of Opponent's Hand Given That He Was Drawing to 8765 or Better and Made an Eight or Better

Your Hand	Probability That His Hand Is Better
8765A	94%
8762A	81%
8752A	70%
8742A	65%
8652A	52%
8642A	47%
8532A	40%
8432A	38%
7652A	27%
7632A	20%
7532A	13%
7432A	11%
6532A	4%
6432A	2%
5432A	

TABLE 6.17b
Distribution of Opponent's Hand Given That He Was Drawing to 8642 or Better and Made an Eight or Better

Your Hand	Probability That His Hand Is Better
8765A	98%
8762A	93%
8752A	87%
8742A	83%
8652A	74%
8642A	65%
8532A	55%
8432A	53%
7652A	38%
7632A	28%
7532A	18%
7432A	15%
6532A	5%
6432A	2%
5432A	

TABLE 6.17c
Distribution of Opponent's Hand Given That He Was Drawing to 7654 or Better and Made a Seven or Better

Your Hand	Probability That His Hand Is Better
7652A	75%
7632A	55%
7532A	35%
7432A	30%
6532A	10%
6432A	5%
5432A	

TABLE 6.17d
Distribution of Opponent's Hand Given That He Was Drawing
to 742A or Better and Made a Seven or Better

Your Hand	Probability That His Hand Is Better
7652A	90%
7632A	78%
7532A	66%
7432A	60%
6532A	20%
6432A	10%
5432A	

7

STUD POKER

In this chapter, I will discuss Five-, Six-, and Seven-Card Stud for high, and also for low. This chapter is meant, in some sense, for the more advanced player, because Stud Poker is substantially more complicated than Draw. There are a sufficient number of different possible upcard combinations and different betting limits so that it is virtually impossible to present strategy tables applicable to more than a few situations. However, it is possible to explain *how* different situations may be analyzed, although it may not be feasible to actually analyze all of them. My treatment will therefore require a little more thought, but it should be extremely rewarding.

Stud games for huge stakes are not uncommon. For example, there have been pots won in Five-Card Stud that contained over $10,000. One of the popular games in Nevada is Seven-Card Stud for low, also known as Razz. This game is occasionally played with a $100 limit for the first few rounds, and a $200 limit toward the end.

Before each game is analyzed individually, several topics of general importance will be discussed. These preliminary sections should not be skipped since they will be basic to our later discussion.

LIMITS

Limits in Stud may generally be classified in one of two categories: low limit and high limit. Based on my experience, I would say that the typical low-limit game has a limit that increases slightly and is, on the average, approximately one fourth the size of the total ante. Listed below are several games that fall into this category:

> Game 1: Total ante 8 chips, limit 2 chips on each round.
> Game 2: Total ante 8 chips, limit 1 chip on first round, 2 chips on next two rounds, 3 chips on last round.
> Game 3: Total ante 6 chips, limit 1 chip on first two rounds, 2 chips on last two rounds.

High-limit games are typically played pot limit, table stakes, or with a constant (but high) limit. Since there is a considerable difference between, say, a table stakes game and a game with an 8-chip total ante and a 2-chip limit, I will generally analyze each type of limit separately. It will be convenient throughout the chapter to assume that the limit is bet unless otherwise stated. Thus if the game is pot limit and I say that someone should bet, I will mean that he should bet the pot. When no limit is specified, the reader should assume that all bets equal the pot.

GENERAL CONSIDERATIONS

Three basic considerations pervade all of Stud: upcards, concealment, and position. A player who understands these concepts alone should have an edge in most games.

The upcards that appear about the table are particularly important because they affect everyone's chances of winning.

For example, if you hold 9̲9̲K4* and two nines and a king appear in other hands, you won't be able to make three nines, and you are unlikely to make a full house. In other words, you will have almost no chance of winning. However, if none of your cards appear and several of your opponents' cards show up in other hands, you may actually be a favorite. It is clear, then, that it will pay you to watch for the cards that most affect your hand. By doing so you should find it easier to remember other cards as well.

Concealment is of concern primarily in high-limit games, where the main objective should be to win a big pot. By a concealed hand I mean a hand like QQ5 as opposed to Q5Q, or a hand like K̲2 as opposed to 2̲K. It's hard to make a good hand with something like Q5Q without showing your strength. If you catch a five you will have queens up, but this hand is almost as likely to lose a big pot as it is to win one. If you catch a queen you will probably scare out your opposition. Consequently, although Q5Q may win more small pots than JJ3, it is unlikely to win as many big ones, and it is therefore somewhat inferior as far as table stakes play is concerned. The same kind of criticism can be made of a hand like 3̲K as opposed to Q2.

We saw in the Draw chapters that position has a profound effect on strategy in Draw, and it has a similar effect in Stud. A player with good position can bet with weaker hands because his opponents will have shown weakness by checking. Similarly, he can call with weaker hands because he will have fewer players behind him.

READING HANDS

In order to read hands in Stud, you should consider your opponents' upcards, the way they have bet, and any tells they may have. One trick that I find most useful is just to ask myself whether the player in question initially called or bet. If he called, he probably started with a good hand;

---

* A line under a card means that it is a hole card.

if he bet, he may have started with anything. As an example, consider a game of pot limit Five-Card Stud, in which the initial upcards are 2, 7, 10, 8, K, 9, 4. The king bets. In this case, since he has the best upcard, he may be betting just to win the antes, and he may have nothing in the hole.

Now consider a slightly different situation in which someone else bets with ?A and the player with ?K calls. Here you should figure the player with ?K to have at least a jack in the hole since he cannot steal the pot as he could before. This type of observation can make a big difference when your opponent ends up with something like ?K7QA and you have to decide whether or not he is paired.

A player who makes an early raise generally does not have a really good hand, because the natural reaction with a really good hand is to keep people in. A player who checks after making a sequence of bets will also generally be weak. If you bet after he checks, you will often win the pot.

Be wary of a good player who calls a large bet when a number of the cards he needs have appeared in other hands. This usually means that he has a good hand already. For example, suppose that a good player shows ??J3 in pot limit. On the second round two jacks and a three appear in other hands. However, he still calls a pot-size bet. This is clearly a mistake if he has something like 9JJ3 or 93J3, since he has almost no way to improve these hands. Consequently, there is a strong inference that he holds something like AA3J or even 333J.

In Low Stud* a player who folds with something like ??462 figures to have gotten paired by the last deuce (why else would he drop after catching such a good card?). This observation can be used to keep track of the number of deuces that are left in the deck. If a player calls a pot-size bet with something like ??64K when you show something like ??652, he figures to be drawing smooth. Consequently, an eight will almost certainly help him whereas a deuce may not.

---

* Low Stud is played just like High Stud except that the best low hand wins the pot.

EXERCISES IN READING HANDS ————————————

Problem: The following deal took place in 1965 in Reno, Nevada. The game is table stakes Five-Card Stud. You are playing against an elderly woman who calls each of your increasingly large bets. On the final round you have A̲QQxA and she shows ?̲8Qx8. What do you do?

Answer: There are only two hands she could possibly have to warrant her call when you had two queens showing. She either has three eights or queens up. While her calling with 8̲8Q versus ?̲QQ would be quite questionable, it is also true that her calling with Q8 versus ?̲Q would be questionable. Consequently, there is no reason to assume that queens up is significantly more likely than three eights. The correct play, therefore, is to check.

In the actual contest, the woman raised (she had three eights), and her opponent called, which was another mistake. He lost his entire stack.

Problem: A conservative and mediocre opponent faces you in Seven-Card Stud, showing ?̲?̲10 2 4 J in different suits. You hold QQ10 10 8 K. On preceding rounds you bet and he called. He now raises you the limit of $5. There is $30 in the pot. What do you do?

Answer: Your opponent, being conservative, has not stayed in this long in hope of bluffing you out. He must have at least two pairs. However, the best two pairs he could have would be jacks and tens, a hand that is extremely unlikely and also not worth a raise. We can conclude that he must have three of a kind. Hence you need a full house to win, and this chance is so small that you should drop.

Problem: In Five-Card Stud for low, you hold 7̲4 3 7 and your rather straightforward opponent shows ?̲2̲4 5. After enthusiastically betting the limit on two occasions, he now checks. The limit is $4 this round and there is $12 in the pot. What should you do?

Answer: The situation isn't completely clear-cut, but it looks like your opponent's last card paired him. In this case he will probably retire if you bet, so you should do so. It is important to realize that this play might fail, but it only has to succeed more than 1 time in 4 to show a profit.

CALLING RULES FOR LOW-LIMIT GAMES*

Most calling decisions in high-limit games boil down to a matter of reading hands. If, after estimating your opponent's hand as accurately as possible, you decide that yours is probably inferior, you drop. Otherwise you call. In high limit your pot odds will rarely be sufficient to warrant calling with an obviously inferior hand.

The same is not true, however, in low limit. You may have your opponent read perfectly for A65, and you may hold KQJ. In this case you are obviously an underdog, but your pot odds may warrant a call.

In low limit there will often be a critical point at which you will have to decide whether you will get out or remain on till the end. In these situations you should (a) estimate your chances by looking at either Table 7.2, 7.4, 7.5, or 7.8, and then (b) weigh those chances against the odds offered by the pot. For example, suppose you estimate that you will have to pay $5 to reach a showdown, and that if you win, you will gain $10. In this case you are getting odds of 10 to 5 or 2 to 1, so you need at least a 1 in 3 chance to call. If Tables 7.2, 7.4, 7.5, and 7.8 indicate that you have such a chance, then you should call. Otherwise you should drop.

In general, calling decisions may be broken down into three steps:

1. Estimate the amount you will have to pay to reach a showdown
2. Use this information to calculate the chances you need to call

---

* This section is fairly difficult but it must be read if one wishes to solve the problems given later on in the chapter.

3. Ask yourself whether your actual chances are greater than the chances you need

Step 1 requires a minimum of mathematics. If you wish to perform the calculations in step 2, assume that all the players presently in the pot stay in till the end. In other words, if a showdown figures to cost 8 chips and you have three opponents, assume that each opponent will contribute 8 more chips to the pot. (See Figure 7.1.) If there were 8 chips in the pot at the beginning of the round, you stand to win $4 \times 8 = 32$ chips at a risk of 8 chips. These are odds of 4 to 1, so you need at least a 1 in 5 (20%) chance to call.

FIGURE 7.1
Estimated Contributions of Each Player to the Final Pot

Chips Initially in Pot	Player 1	Player 2	Player 3	You
8 chips	8 chips	8 chips	8 chips	8 chips

Because the computations in step 2 are rather cumbersome, I have included the following rule, which essentially does the computations for you. It may look formidable, but it is actually quite simple. If you can estimate how much you will have to pay to reach a showdown, it will tell you what your chances should be to warrant a call.

RULE 7.1a: Suppose that after you call and others call, there will be n players in the pot. If you estimate that a showdown will cost k times what was in the pot at the beginning of the round, then your chances should be at least $\frac{k}{1 + nk}$ to warrant a call.

EXAMPLE OF USE ─────────────────────────

Let's apply Rule 7.1a to the previous example. There are four players in the pot, a showdown will cost 8 chips, and the pot contained 8 chips at the beginning of the round.

What should your chances be to warrant a call?

Answer: In this case the cost of a showdown equals the amount that was in the pot at the beginning of the round. Therefore $k = 1$. Plugging $k = 1$ and $n = 4$ into Rule 7.1a, we see that your chances should be at least $\frac{1}{1 + 4 \cdot 1} = \frac{1}{5} = $ 20%. This is the same figure that we got before.

It is useful to observe that in order to use the approach outlined by 1, 2, and 3, you must have a fairly good idea as to how much it will cost you to reach a showdown. You do not need to know your actual chances, only whether they are larger or smaller than the chances required to call.

Occasionally you may know your actual chances but you may not know how much a showdown will cost. In this case the following rule will be more convenient to use than Rule 7.1a. It tells you the maximum amount you should pay to reach a showdown when you know what your chances are.

RULE 7.1b: Suppose that after you call and others call, there will be n players in the pot. If your probability of winning is x, then you should call whenever x is at least $1/n$. If x is less than $1/n$, then you should call if the cost of reaching a showdown will not exceed $\frac{x}{1 - nx}$ times what was in the pot at the beginning of the round.

EXAMPLE OF USE: ──────────────────────

Suppose that your Five-Card Stud game has a total ante of 8 chips and a limit of 2 chips. Someone opens for 2 chips and two others call. You are last to speak and hold $\underline{2}$A. In this situation you have roughly a 20% chance of winning. (I will explain how this figure was computed in a subsequent section.) What do you do?

Answer: Here $x = .20$ and $n = 4$. The pot contained 8 chips at the beginning of the round. Plugging $n = 4$ and $x = .20$ into Rule 7.1b, we see that you should call if the cost of reaching a showdown will not exceed $\dfrac{.20}{1-4(.20)}$ × (8 chips) = 8 chips. Since there are four rounds of betting, it seems reasonable that a showdown should cost around 8 chips (four rounds of betting at 2 chips a round). If this is the case, then $\underline{2}$ A is a minimum call. (We should note at this point that there is little difference between opening and calling in low limit. Consequently, if $\underline{2}$ A is a minimum calling hand, it will also be a minimum opening hand.)

FIVE-CARD STUD

OPENING STRATEGY

High Limit

Most Five-Card Stud games have a small ante, or a rule that forces the high man to make a minimum bet. When the rules call for an ante, opening requirements should decrease slightly as one's position improves, but not too much because sandbagging is common in these games.

In general, the number of hands that you can open and play profitably will depend to a large extent on your ability. After all, there is not a great deal of difference between $\underline{K}$ 10 and $\underline{J}$ 9. A good player will win money with both of them. However, since the size of the antes relative to the total amounts wagered in pot limit is so small, it can hardly hurt to play tight.

My view in high limit is that the objective should be to win a big pot, and this is best accomplished by (a) starting out with a pair or (b) making a concealed high pair on either the second or third upcard. If you start with $\underline{2}$ A, you may make an exposed pair of aces or a concealed pair of deuces, but in one case you will get no action and in the other case it will be hard to bet. With a hand like K 8 K 10 or 3 3 8 8 you figure to win, and you can also build a pot. Consequently, I prefer to play pairs, or hands with a high hole card. As far as hands like ? A are concerned, I prefer to play them provided I have at least a nine in the hole. This way, my opponents know I am strong when I show an ace, and they are running scared. Playing all aces is weak because one is in a bad position at the second upcard. If you bet, you are getting deeper into the pot with a potential loser; and if you check, your opponents figure to start betting. When I bet with ? A and catch a 10, my opponents already fear that I am paired, and I have a good chance of winning on a bluff. Furthermore, with J A 10 I have a reasonable call after checking.

The following table may be of interest in that it gives an idea of what to expect from various numbers of opponents. For example, in an eight-man game, someone else figures to have a pair 35% of the time (bottom row, column 7).

TABLE 7.1

Probability That an Opponent Has a Pair or a Hole Card of at Least a	Number of Opponents						
	1	2	3	4	5	6	7
Q	30%	51%	66%	75%	83%	88%	92%
K	22%	39%	53%	63%	71%	77%	82%
A	14%	26%	36%	45%	53%	60%	65%
pairing card	6%	12%	17%	22%	27%	31%	35%

Low Limit

Because there tends to be quite a lot of competition in low limit, the important opening consideration should be your chances of winning in a showdown. For this purpose, K Q will be a significantly better starting hand than A 2, simply because ace high is not going to win the final pot; it will take at least a medium pair. If there are four contestants in the pot who figure to stay till the end, the average winning hand will be around a pair of queens. Consequently, aces, kings, and queens will be the cards of real value, and of course, any pair.

In order to get a feel for what the minimum opening hands should be in a seven-man game, I dealt out nine sets of seven hands and took the best four hands from each set. These four hands were then dealt out, in their entirety, 10,000 times. The frequency with which various hands won is shown in entries 15 through 23 of Table 7.2.

Some of the entries, like entry 22, may look funny because they show A5 doing better than AJ. This is because two other hands in entry 22 also contain jacks.

TABLE 7.2
Chances of Winning in a Variety of Contests
(Five-Card Stud)

Entry	Hand 1	Hand 2	Hand 3	Hand 4
1	22 66.4%*	A6 33.6%		
2	JJ 74.1%	AQ 25.9%		
3	226 70.0%	A87 30.0%		
4	1010 82.3%	A6 17.7%		
5	1010 77.0%	22 23.0%		
6	A2 62.0%	KQ 38.0%		
7	K5 57.2%	Q5 42.8%		
8	QQ 71.1%	A6 14.8%	K7 14.1%	

* Probability of winning in a showdown.

TABLE 7.2 (Continued)

Entry	Hand 1	Hand 2	Hand 3	Hand 4
9	88 65.6%	A6 17.7%	K7 16.7%	
10	22 45.9%	A6 26.8%	K7 27.3%	
11	88 52.2%	A6 17.8%	K7 16.6%	Q4 13.4%
12	22 36.9%	A6 23.7%	K7 21.4%	Q4 18.0%
13	QQ 55.5%	A6 12.2%	K7 10.5%	88 21.8%
14	QQ3 53.8%	66A 22.3%	K72 7.4%	883 16.4%
15	A2 27.9%	KJ 25.3%	K8 23.5%	K7 23.3%
16	A8 22.3%	A2 19.7%	K10 33.0%	Q7 25.0%
17	A10 29.6%	K7 24.5%	Q9 23.9%	Q6 22.0%
18	K7 29.1%	J10 22.6%	Q2 28.1%	105 20.2%
19	66 41.2%	A4 17.9%	K10 22.3%	J7 18.6%
20	22 40.3%	KJ 23.4%	K9 18.3%	109 18.0%
21	QQ 52.8%	1010 22.6%	AK 15.7%	A2 8.9%
22	AJ 25.1%	A5 27.0%	J4 24.0%	J2 23.9%
23	K5 26.6%	J7 27.9%	106 23.3%	104 22.2%

The average percentage of time that an ace and a small card win in the contests is 20%. The same average for KJ or K10 is 25%. Since a minimum opening hand needs at least a 20% chance (see example on pages 138–139), then we can conclude that $\underline{2}$A, $\underline{7}$K, and $\underline{10}$Q all represent minimum opening hands. A pair of deuces, however, is considerably better than minimum. In entries 19 and 20, the small pair wins an average of 40.7% of the time.

One author has actually claimed, by the way, that $\underline{K}$Q is a significantly better starting hand than a low pair, and that $\underline{K}$Q should raise whereas a low pair should not. His argument is based on the fact that $\underline{K}$Q figures to improve about 39% of the time to a hand of at least queens, whereas $\underline{2}$2 only figures to improve about 29% of the time. I agree with these statements. But which would the author rather have when he *does* improve, a pair of kings, or either two pairs or three of a kind? As you can see from entries 19 and 20 of Table 7.2, it's not even close.

CALLING STRATEGY FOR THE FIRST ROUND

High Limit

Against one player who has opened for the size of the pot, it is generally wrong to call with less than an even chance of winning in a showdown. If, for example, the hand were completely dealt out and you actually did have an even chance, you would end up winning, on the average, about half of the total ante. However, you might have to risk many times that, and furthermore, you can't be sure that someone behind you won't have a better hand. This analysis implies, for one thing, that it is usually wrong to call when beaten in sight, for your chances in these instances will typically be around 40%. It also implies that you should generally not call a tight player with less than a pair.

To understand why this is so, suppose your opponent is known to open only with a pair, an ace, or a king. He cur-

rently shows ?10. You hold A̲K. This hand looks good; in
fact, some players might even raise. But entry 2 of Table
7.2 indicates that you will only have a 26% chance when your
opponent has tens, and entry 6 indicates that your chances
won't be much over 62% when he has A̲10 or K̲10. Your
overall chances will therefore be almost exactly even. Hence
with a lesser hand than A̲K you might be well advised to
drop.

In actual play, of course, it is also necessary to consider
how your opponent figures to play on subsequent rounds.
If he is easily bluffed, then it may be right to play somewhat
weaker hands with an eye toward bluffing. This is all part of
the game.

Low Limit

The requirements for calling in low limit have already
been discussed. Examples of minimum calls are 2̲A, 7̲K, and
10̲Q. These requirements should be tightened slightly if
cards that you need appear in other hands. For example,
if the other upcards are 7, K, 10, 8, Q, J, then you should
drop with 10̲Q or 7̲K because a Q, 10, K, and 7 appear, but
you can call with 2̲A.

RAISING STRATEGY FOR THE FIRST ROUND

This section concerns only low-limit games, because raising in high limit is more a matter of psychology than anything else.

The classic question in low-limit games is whether one
should raise with a small pair on the first round. A raise
figures to thin out the competition, but is this really advantageous? The answer is yes, primarily because a raise will
increase your chances of winning the large pot which exists
at the time the raise is made. Consider, for example, a situation in which you start with 2̲2 against an A̲6, K̲7, and Q̲4.

(This is entry 12 of Table 7.2.) Each time everyone puts a bet in the pot, you figure to win an additional .48 of a bet.* If you raise and knock one opponent out, you will be left in a situation similar to entry 10, in which your average gain per bet is about .38. If you knock two out, you will be left in a situation similar to entry 1, in which your average gain per bet is about .33. Since these figures decrease, there is little if any value in raising when the pot is small. It is only because the pot will usually be large in low-limit that it is right to raise.

THE PLAY OF AN OPEN PAIR

Since the play of an open pair is much more important in high limit, I will restrict my attention here to this type of game.

Intermediate-Round Play

When someone bets the pot with an open pair, anyone who can't beat the pair should drop. A player who can beat the pair should attempt to read his opponents' hands and then use his judgment.

When you hold the open pair, there are three cases to consider.

1. You have concealed strength and want to keep your opponents in the pot.
2. You aren't sure whether anyone has you beat but you don't want to let anyone draw for free.
3. You are fairly certain that someone has you beat and you want to scare them out or get to draw without paying a lot of money.

---

* This figure was derived as follows: For the additional bet you put in, you figure to get back four bets 36.9% of the time (entry 12, Table 7.2). Therefore your average gain per bet is $.369(4) - 1 \approx .48$.

In all situations your play should be varied to confuse your opponents, but most of your bets should be made to maximize your gain. For example, suppose you are in situation 2. In this case you should check occasionally and bet the limit occasionally, but most of your bets should be just large enough so that everyone with an inferior hand will drop. This way, you'll win the pot if everyone has an inferior hand, and you won't be risking more than you have to. A good bet under these circumstances is one third of the pot. This gives your opponents odds of 4 to 1. They usually need odds of at least 6 to 1 in order to call with an inferior hand.

In situation 1, your most frequent bets should be of two types, either the limit or a bet that is small enough to keep almost everyone in. Your choice should depend on whether you feel that a number of players have pairs higher than your showing pair, in which case they will probably call the larger bet. To keep your opponents confused, occasionally make the same size bet you would normally make if you found yourself in situation 2.

Your play in situation 3 should depend on what your opponents think you have. For example, suppose you have a reputation for being conservative, but have entered the pot with 10J, which developed into 10JKJ. In this case an expert opponent with aces might well put you on three jacks, or kings and jacks, and he may fold if you bet the limit. If you don't like your chances of bluffing everyone out, bet a small amount (like you would do in situation 1). Your opponents won't know whether you have a cinch or not, so they probably won't raise.

Final-Round Play

If your open pair is all you have at this point (let's say that your hand is K8Q87), you should not bet with the expectation of making more money. Anyone who calls you can see your open pair and will therefore have a better hand. The only bets you make in this situation should be bluffs. Indeed, the fact that your opponents called on the last round when they could see your open pair almost certainly means that you will have to bluff if you want to win.

As far as the play of a cinch is concerned, there are two possibilities.

CASE 1: You showed an open pair prior to the fifth card, i.e., you: K̲ 10 8 10 K, opponent: ? Q 3 A 4.

In this case your opponent's call on the previous round indicated that he could beat tens. To emphasize this point, I'm going to turn his hole card faceup: A̲ Q 3 A 4. You can't really expect someone to bet into you when his whole hand is exposed. Therefore you must bet. He won't know whether this bet is a bluff or not, so he may very well call.

CASE 2: You received your open pair on the last card, i.e., you: K̲ 10 K 8 10, opponent: ? Q 3 A 4.

Here your correct strategy should depend on the frequency with which your opponent bluffs. If he bluffs a lot, you should check. Against a good player, however, your best strategy is to bet most of the time. Without giving a detailed reason for this, I will merely point out that the last ten that you catch is a very intimidating card. Before catching this card you apparently felt that you had a good chance of winning. After catching this card your hand improves considerably, and it is a little too much to ask that your opponent now bet into you so that you can raise. In other words, you are the one who should do most of the betting in this situation.

CALLING STRATEGY FOR INTERMEDIATE ROUNDS

High Limit

In high limit it virtually never pays to call with an inferior hand, except possibly with the intention of bluffing. If you have to call two pot-size bets to have a showdown, you will be risking four times the initial pot in the hope of winning five times the initial pot. These are odds of only 5 to 4. Inferior hands typically need odds of at least 2 to 1 in order to call.

Probably the most common legitimate problem occurs when one player shows an open pair and another player has a higher concealed pair. If the player with the open pair plays tight, the chances of his having another pair or trips will typically be between $\frac{1}{3}$ and $\frac{1}{2}$. When they are $\frac{1}{2}$ or over, a concealed higher pair should generally be dropped. To see this, suppose that we hold 9̲925 against a tight player who shows ?̲J66. Let's assume that he has an even chance of having a jack in the hole, and that he would bet the pot in either event. He bets the pot of $10. At this point we are getting 2 to 1 odds on an even-money proposition, so it looks like a call is in order. However, this is not the whole story. The problem is that we may also have to call on the next round.* If our opponent has a cinch, he's going to bet $30 on the next round, and we're going to have to call him roughly half of the time to keep him honest.** This will cost us, on the average, half of a $30 bet, or $15 in addition to the $10 already put in. When he does not have a cinch, one of two things will happen: He will either check or bluff. If he checks, there is no point in our betting, since our call indicated that we could beat his board. Our gain in this case will be $20 (the $10 initially in the pot plus the $10 that he bet). If he bluffs and we call half of the time, it can be shown that we will also win, on the average, $20. The conclusion is that we figure to lose $25 when he has a cinch, whereas we figure to gain only $20 when he does not. Therefore we should drop.

Low Limit

In low limit it is often right to call with a slightly inferior hand, but it is generally wrong to call an open pair without a higher concealed pair. However, there are exceptions. Suppose you hold K̲J98 against a player who shows ?̲J77. There are 3 kings, 2 jacks, 3 nines, and 3 eights, or 11 cards out of 45 that will enable you to beat sevens. Thus your

---

* For simplicity, let's neglect the small chance that someone improves.
** Rule 9.4 of Chapter 9.

chances of beating sevens are close to 1 in 4, so your overall
chances of winning are probably at least 1 in 6. This means
you would have a call if your pot odds were over 5 to 1, and
they often will be in low limit.

The same type of analysis may be applied to situations in
which neither player shows a pair. Suppose this time that
you hold K̲Q J 2 and your opponent shows ?̲K 5 A. Here an
ace may win for you, as well as any pair, so there are 14 cards
out of 45 that may win. If your opponent plays loosely, you
may have close to a 1 in 4 chance.

SIX- AND SEVEN-CARD STUD

OPENING REQUIREMENTS

Opening requirements should depend on the limit, the
ante, and the number of players in the game. Listed below
are *potentially* playable hands. The list includes hands like
draws to straights and flushes which should be *played* but
not opened. When you hold a draw to a straight or a flush,
you should prefer to check in the hope that everyone else
will check and you can then see your fourth card free.

The ranking was done for low-limit Seven-Card Stud.
Draws to straights and flushes are less appealing in Six-
Card Stud and in high-limit games. The problem with such
hands in high-limit games is that your opponents can make
it very expensive to draw.

1. Best hands   Three of a kind
                                 Three cards to a straight flush
                                 Three high cards to a flush
                                 Concealed pair of aces or kings

2. Good hands   Unconcealed pair of aces or kings
                             Concealed pair of queens or jacks
                             Three high cards to an open-end
                               straight (Q J 10)
                             Three cards to a flush

3. Fair hands   Unconcealed pair of queens or jacks
                             Unconcealed pair below jacks with a
                               high kicker (4 K 4)
                             Concealed pair below jacks
                             Three cards to an open-end straight
                               (7 6 5)

4. Questionable hands   Unconcealed pair below jacks
                             Three high cards (K J 9)
                             Two high cards with a two flush
                               (♥A ♣Q ♣7)

High Limit

In high limit your worst opening hands in a bad position should be something like 2 2 K, 9 9 5, and 4 J J. (These requirements may be reduced slightly if you are betting less than the pot.) To vary your play, you should also open occasionally with hands like 2 K 2, ♣4 ♣8 ♣Q, and 9 10 J.

In a good position your requirements should depend on the amount of sandbagging that is done. If players rarely sandbag, you can open with any pair in a good position.

Table 7.3 may be of interest since it gives an idea of what

TABLE 7.3
Probabilities of Initial Hands

Hand	Approximate Probability
Three of a kind	¼%
Three cards to a straight flush	⅓%
Any three cards to a flush	5%
Any three cards to a straight	4%
Concealed pair	6%
Unconcealed pair	12%
Any pair	18%

to expect from a particular opponent. For example, if a
player shows ??K, Table 7.3 indicates that he will have a
pair of kings 12% of the time, a concealed pair 6% of the
time, and a straight or flush draw 9% of the time.

Low Limit

In order to get a feel for what the minimum opening
hands should be in a low-limit seven-man game, I used
essentially the same techniques used for Five-Card Stud.
Twenty sets of seven hands were dealt out, and the four best
hands from each set were matched against one another.
The results of six of the more representative contests are
shown in entries 32 through 37 of Table 7.4.

If we average out how small pairs with low kickers do in
the contests, we find that they win about 23% of the time.
Similarly, hands with two high cards and one low one win
about 17% of the time. As we indicated, a minimum opening
hand should win about 20% of the time. Therefore we can
conclude that it is correct to open with any pair. With two
high cards it is a good idea to have something extra, like
two cards in suit. Examples of borderline opening hands are
♥A♣Q♣7 and KJ9.

TABLE 7.4
Chances of Winning in a Variety of Contests
(Six- and Seven-Card Stud)

Entry		Hand 1	Hand 2	Hand 3	Hand 4
		225	A108		
1	6-Card Stud	63.4%*	36.6%		
2	7-Card Stud	58.8%	41.2%		
		2275	88A10		
3	6-Card Stud	25.6%	74.4%		
4	7-Card Stud	33.2%	66.8%		
		22KJ	88106		
5	6-Card Stud	32.6%	67.4%		
6	7-Card Stud	45.3%	54.7%		

* Probability of winning in a showdown.

TABLE 7.4 (Continued)

Entry		Hand 1	Hand 2	Hand 3	Hand 4
		KK2	883		
7	6-Card Stud	70.0%	30.0%		
8	7-Card Stud	65.7%	34.3%		
		6622	A1088		
9	6-Card Stud	69.1%	30.9%		
10	7-Card Stud	57.3%	42.7%		
		6622	A1084		
11	7-Card Stud	84.6%	15.4%		
		JJ66	88A10		
12	6-Card Stud	82.6%	17.4%		
13	7-Card Stud	72.8%	27.2%		
		7779	22KJ		
14	6-Card Stud	98.8%	1.2%		
15	7-Card Stud	96.5%	3.5%		
		7779	88KJ		
16	6-Card Stud	91.8%	8.2%		
17	7-Card Stud	86.3%	13.7%		
		995	A108	Q J6	
18	6-Card Stud	56.8%	22.1%	21.1%	
19	7-Card Stud	51.7%	25.3%	23.0%	
		KK5	A108	Q J6	
20	6-Card Stud	75.1%	16.2%	8.7%	
21	7-Card Stud	66.6%	20.3%	13.1%	
		KK5	88A	Q J6	
22	6-Card Stud	59.5%	33.8%	6.7%	
23	7-Card Stud	53.4%	37.9%	8.7%	
		JJ66	88A10	55Q6	
24	6-Card Stud	61.8%	19.9%	18.3%	
25	7-Card Stud	52.9%	26.1%	21.0%	

TABLE 7.4 (Continued)

Entry		Hand 1	Hand 2	Hand 3	Hand 4
		6622	A1084	55Q6	
26	6-Card Stud	68.9%	6.0%	25.1%	
27	7-Card Stud	52.2%	14.8%	33.0%	
		55J2	8864	33K9	
28	6-Card Stud	25.4%	43.7%	30.9%	
29	7-Card Stud	28.3%	33.3%	38.4%	
		55KQ	66A10	JJ43	
30	6-Card Stud	27.2%	29.2%	43.6%	
31	7-Card Stud	32.6%	33.3%	34.1%	
		22A	QJ3	KJ7	A93
32	7-Card Stud	43.1%	16.6%	21.6%	18.7%
		KK9	88K	QJ3	A54
33	7-Card Stud	44.5%	27.2%	11.4%	16.9%
		JJ2	10105	AJ2	A52
34	7-Card Stud	40.8%	36.3%	11.3%	11.6%
		JJ4	447	332	A97
35	7-Card Stud	36.3%	20.1%*	28.0%	15.6%
		KJ8	Q43	J95	1092
36	7-Card Stud	30.5%	26.8%	20.6%	22.1%
		AA6	994	226	KQ5
37	7-Card Stud	42.9%	26.3%	19.8%	11.0%

* This entry is lower than that for the 332 because a 7 and a 4 appear in the other hands.

FIRST-ROUND CALLING STRATEGY

High Limit

Calling requirements in high limit should depend on the position of the opener. Hands that will always warrant a call are 2̲2̲K, 1̲0̲1̲0̲5, ♣2̲♣5̲♣Q, and ♣1̲0̲♦J♥Q. Your objective with all of these hands should be to look at your fourth card. If it doesn't help in any way and someone bets, you should generally drop. If it does help, you may win a big pot. The purpose of the ♣Q and ♥Q as upcards is to prevent your opponents from easily reading you. If you call 2 pot-size bets with something like ??♣3♣8, for example, your opponents will almost always read you for a four flush. They can make it very expensive to draw, and they will drop the minute they see you've made your hand.

As far as calling with unconcealed pairs is concerned, you should generally have either an ace in the hole or a higher upcard than the player who bet. In other words, if a reasonably tight player bets the pot with ??J, then you need at least 2A2 or xQQ to call. With a hand like x1010, you figure to be beaten, and you also have little chance of winning a big pot.

Low Limit

First-round calling requirements in low limit are about the same as the opening requirements. The following are minimum calls: KJ9, ♥A♣Q♣7, and 232. These requirements may be reduced if your game is shorthanded or if it has an exceptionally large ante. As usual, you should watch for cards that affect your hand. For example, if the other upcards are K, J, 3, 8, 9, 2, then you should drop with KJ9 or 232 but you can call with ♥A♣Q♣7.

STRATEGIES FOR INTERMEDIATE ROUNDS

High Limit

Good betting and calling strategies for high limit essentially consist of (a) reading hands and then (b) making intelligent use of that information. Consequently, little can be said mathematically, and the best I can do is give an example of the kinds of thinking involved.

EXAMPLE

Suppose in Seven-Card Stud that you hold Q̲Q̲K10 10 against a good player who shows ??J2J, the first jack and deuce being of different suits. He has called 2 pot-size bets in succession, and now checks. What action do you take?

Answer: Two questions should be asked. What does he have, and what does he think you have? Since the jack and deuce are off-color, he almost certainly wasn't drawing to a straight or a flush. Would he have called a pot-size bet with something like a 5̲5̲J2 against your ??K10? Most good players wouldn't, so it looks like he started with something like A̲A̲J or x̲JJ, and the second hand is more likely. In either case, it is clear that you should check. He probably has put you on two pairs and is hoping that you will continue to bet.

Low Limit

In low-limit games some understanding of the relevant mathematics will be useful because, for one thing, it will often be right to call when obviously behind. A good approach for handling calling questions consists of (a) reading hands and using Table 7.4 to approximate your chances and then (b) applying either Rule 7.1a or 7.1b. The first problem given below is an example of the use of this technique.

PROBLEM

In Seven-Card Stud you hold 9̲9̲A10 while your opponents show ??66 and ??55. You believe that one player probably has two pairs or trips. Using entry 25 of Table

7.4, you estimate your chances of winning at about 20%. The pot contained $7 at the beginning of the round and the limit is $1. The player with sixes bets the limit and your other opponent calls. What do you do?

Answer: Rule 7.1a says to call if it won't cost more than $\frac{.20}{1 - 3(.20)} \times (\$7) = \$3.50$ to have a showdown. Since there are three rounds after this one, that looks like a pretty good estimate of what it will cost. Therefore your correct play is a toss-up.

PROBLEM ─────────────────────────────────

You hold 6̲2̲26 in a shorthanded Seven-Card Stud game against a carefree opponent who shows ??A4. There is $5 in the pot and you're playing $3 limit. Should you make a large bet or a small one?

Answer: If your opponent has a pair, entry 10 of Table 7.4 rates your chances at about 57%. In this case it won't matter much whether you bet the limit or not, since you'll be only slightly favored. If he doesn't have a pair, entry 11 of Table 7.4 gives you about an 85% chance. Now you definitely want to keep him in, so you should probably make a moderate bet of around $1.50.

FINAL-ROUND STRATEGY

In a low-limit game it will always pay to bet when you think you have the best hand, because your opponents will almost always call to protect their interests. The same is not true in high limit, however, because players will frequently not call pot-size bets. Therefore the real consideration in a high-limit game should be the amount of time you will be called and will win, rather than just your chances of winning.

The following problem illustrates the use of this kind of reasoning.

PROBLEM ───

You hold K̲K̲8 J A8 5̲ and your opponent shows ?̲?̲ 10 6 J 2 ?̲, the 10 and 6 being spades. He has called 4 pot-size bets in succession. What do you do?

Answer: The only conceivable hand your opponent could call with and lose would be two pairs. However, his most likely initial holding was three flush cards, and if he started with such a hand, he almost certainly won't call if he misses on the last card. Initial holdings like 10̲ J 10 and Q̲Q̲ 10 might leave him with two pairs, but these are unlikely, and there's no guarantee he will call when he has such hands. It looks like your chances of getting called and winning are smaller than your chances of getting called or raised and losing, so don't bet.

SIX- AND SEVEN-CARD STUD FOR LOW

Six- and Seven-Card Stud for low are fairly new poker forms that deserve considerable attention. They are closely related to Six- and Seven-Card Stud for high and low, which are discussed in the next chapter. A good general rule for Six-Card Stud is to open and call with any three low cards to an eight or better. This requirement should be reduced in a low-limit game and whenever most players show bad up-cards.

Since a seven will frequently be made in Seven-Card Stud, it is generally a bad idea to get into a big pot with an eight in your hand. However, you must play with eights and even with nines on occasion. Otherwise you will be labeled as being too "tight" and you will get little action.

When your starting hand is 765 or better, you should generally not raise in a loose game, because such a hand does best with many players in the pot. To see this, notice that 765 has a 52.2% chance in entry 20 of Table 7.5, while 73A has only a 60.9% chance in entry 8. In other words, 765 improves its chances by less than 9% when it drives out a mediocre competitor. This improvement should be more like 25% to make such an action profitable.

TABLE 7.5
Chances of Winning in a Variety of Contests
(Six- and Seven-Card Stud for Low)

Entry		Hand 1	Hand 2	Hand 3
		62A	876	
1	6-Card Stud	55.7%*	44.3%	
2	7-Card Stud	60.4%	39.6%	
		652A	8765	
3	6-Card Stud	65.5%	34.5%	
4	7-Card Stud	71.0%	29.0%	
		K432A	98542	
5	7-Card Stud	57.3%	42.7%	
		K432A	76543	
6	7-Card Stud	35.5%	64.5%	
		K32	73A	
7	6-Card Stud	28.3%	71.7%	
8	7-Card Stud	39.1%	60.9%	
		K732	754A	
9	6-Card Stud	21.2%	78.8%	
10	7-Card Stud	28.4%	71.6%	

* Probability of winning in a showdown.

TABLE 7.5 (Continued)

Entry		Hand 1	Hand 2	Hand 3
		K732	983A	
11	6-Card Stud	28.4%	71.6%	
12	7-Card Stud	40.0%	60.0%	
		KJ32	K732	
13	6-Card Stud	39.1%	60.9%	
		KQ53	985A	
14	7-Card Stud	13.5%	86.5%	
		K32	876	74A
15	6-Card Stud	11.6%	40.8%	47.6%
16	7-Card Stud	16.2%	32.6%	51.2%
		K763	8765	742A
17	6-Card Stud	9.8%	31.3%	58.9%
18	7-Card Stud	14.4%	25.0%	60.6%
		K43	765	Q42
19	6-Card Stud	18.0%	57.8%	24.2%
20	7-Card Stud	23.6%	52.2%	24.2%
		K632	7653	Q742
21	6-Card Stud	18.1%	65.8%	16.1%
22	7-Card Stud	24.6%	55.7%	19.6%
		K6532	87654	Q7432
23	7-Card Stud	37.1%	30.4%	32.5%
		K6532	98765	Q7432
24	7-Card Stud	48.5%	17.5%	34.0%

READING HANDS

Reading hands is considerably more straightforward in Low Stud than in high because, with rare exceptions, there are only three basic classes of hands a player can have: He can have either zero, one, or two bad cards.

The most important considerations from a purely mathematical point of view are (a) the probability of starting with a low hand and (b) the probability that a player will make a low hand when he catches a number of low cards. Tables 7.6 and 7.7 give these probabilities. Table 7.6 is particularly useful for judging what opponents play with. For example, the figure of 19% besides the 7xx indicates that a player figures to have 765 or better 19% of the time when his upcard is low. Consequently, if you see someone playing about 50% of the time when his upcard is low, you can be sure he's playing with worse hands than 765; in fact, he's probably playing with 10xx's.

TABLE 7.6
Probabilities of Various
Initial Hands
(Assuming a Low Upcard*)

Hand	Probability
10xx or better**	45%
9xx or better	35%
8xx or better	26%
7xx or better	19%
6xx or better	13%

* A "low upcard" means a card seven or below.

** "10xx or better" means any hand 1098 or better. Similarly, "9xx or better" means any hand 987 or better, etc.

Table 7.7 gives the probability that a player will make a hand when he catches a number of good cards. When using the table, it is useful to remember that a player who bets is more likely to be paired than one who calls. For example, suppose that you hold A̲4̲7810 in intermediate-limit Six-Card Stud, and your opponent shows ?̲?̲732. He bets the limit on each round. In this case he may well be betting with a pair of deuces or threes. However, if he called someone else when he held ?̲?̲73, it is likely that the deuce would be the only card that might pair him. We see, then, that in one case his probability of having a hand might be as high as 70% (second row of table), whereas in the other case it would probably be closer to 50% (third row of table).

TABLE 7.7
Probability That an Opponent Makes a Hand When He Catches a Number of Low Cards

	Opponent Starts With	
	7xx or Better	8xx or Better
Probability that the second low upcard does not pair a hole card	73%	77%
Probability that the third low upcard does not pair a hole card, given that the second upcard did not	67%	73%
Probability that an opponent makes a hand when he catches two low upcards	49%	56%
Probability that an opponent makes a hand when he catches three low upcards	73%	90%

GENERAL BETTING STRATEGY

It is never wrong to bet the limit with a slight edge, but you should also check occasionally to vary your play. Many players make the mistake of valuing a made hand too highly. As entry 5 of Table 7.5 points out, a rough nine in five cards is an underdog when competing against four good low cards. Even a rough eight can be an underdog when put up against two smooth draws (entry 23).

The correct play with something like 3̲ 4̲ 7 8 5 9 K̲ is to check when your opponent shows something like ?̲ ?̲ 3 2 K K ?̲. He won't call with worse than a nine, so most of his calls will win.

In a pot-limit expert game, if you show two good cards and your opponent shows something like ?̲ ?̲ 2 9, you have an automatic bet. Your opponent should drop regardless of his hole cards. In general, it is a good idea to bet the limit whenever you have a significant advantage on board, especially in Seven-Card Stud.

The best time to bluff in low limit is when two of your hole cards have to be bad to lose, and they are. However, avoid carrying a bluff too far. If an intelligent opponent has called a number of bets with a significantly inferior board, he probably knows something. In this case further bluffing will be futile.

CALLING STRATEGY

Pot Limit

It doesn't pay to call in pot limit with a significant disadvantage. Examples of minimum calls against a tight player in Six-Card Stud are 5̲6̲78 versus ?̲?̲46, 5̲6̲788 versus ?̲?̲46Q, and 4̲3̲2KA versus ?̲?̲754.* For playing purposes, 5̲6̲78Q is the same as 5̲6̲788 when up against ?̲?̲46Q. You can't call or bet on the next round with worse than a jack, so it doesn't matter whether your odd card is a queen or an eight.

Since 5̲6̲788 represents a borderline call against ?̲?̲46Q, it follows that it represents a call against ?̲?̲46K or ?̲?̲466 and a drop against ?̲?̲46J or ?̲?̲4610.

If you bet 7̲2̲5A against a player showing ?̲?̲78 in Six-Card Stud, you should call if he catches below a seven and you pair fives. True, he is about 2 to 1 favored to have an eight, but you can bet the pot on the next round if you catch a 6, 4, or 3, and you may also be able to bet the pot if you catch an 8.

It is useful to note that Six-Card Stud contests may be transformed into equivalent Seven-Card Stud contests by giving both players a bad card. For example, 5̲6̲78 versus ?̲?̲46 in Six-Card Stud is the same** as 5̲6̲7K8 versus ?̲?̲4K6 in Seven-Card Stud.

---

*In each contest, I assume that the player with the best board bets whether he is paired or not.

**There is actually a slight difference because the last card in Seven-Card Stud is dealt down whereas the last card in Six-Card Stud is dealt up.

Smooth draws (or smooth boards) do better in Seven-Card Stud because they have more opportunity to make a lock, or something that looks like one. Thus while $\underline{5}\underline{6}78$ represents a borderline call against $\underline{?}\underline{?}46$ in Six-Card Stud, it should be dropped in Seven-Card Stud.

Intermediate Limit

In low- and intermediate-limit games, the player with the low board has less of an advantage because he cannot bluff his opponent out as easily as he can in high limit. Many contests in low- and intermediate-limit games go right down to the wire. In these situations Table 7.5 and either Rule 7.1a or 7.1b may be used to good advantage. The following exercises illustrate this approach.

PROBLEM ─────────────────────────────────────

A $10 limit Six-Card Stud game finds you holding $\underline{7}\underline{3}2K$ versus a conservative opponent who shows $\underline{?}\underline{?}98$. He bets the limit. Prior to his bet, there was $15 in the pot. What do you do?

Answer: In this particular situation it is unlikely that the eight paired your opponent. Consequently, let us proceed under the assumption that he holds 98xx. In this case, entry 11 of Table 7.5 gives you about a 28% chance of winning. Using Rule 7.1a with $x = .28$, you should call if it won't cost more than $\frac{.28}{1 - .56} \times \$15 \approx \$9$ to see your opponent's hand. His present bet is $10, so you should definitely drop.

PROBLEM **(hard)** ─────────────────────────────

In $10 limit Seven-Card Stud, you hold $\underline{5}\underline{6}78$, and your tight opponent shows $\underline{?}\underline{?}34$. He bets the limit, as he would always do in this situation. You figure that he started with

7xx or better. There was $20 in the pot before his bet. What do you do?

Answer: Using Table 7.7, he figures to be paired about 27% of the time, in which case we can estimate your chances at about 65% (entries 10 and 12 of Table 7.5). Otherwise, your chances will be around 29% (entry 4 of Table 7.5). Consequently, your overall chances will be roughly $.27(.65) + .73(.29) \approx 40\%$ (chances that he paired, .27; that he didn't pair, .73). Using Rule 7.1b with $x = .40$, we see that a showdown shouldn't cost more than $\frac{.40}{1 - .80} \times$ $20 = 40. That's the most it could cost, so you should call.

FIVE-CARD STUD FOR LOW

The requirements for this game are quite simple. You must have two unpaired low cards, eight or below, to play. Sometimes in low limit it will pay to play when your *hole* card is a nine, because few good lows are made. (The average winning hand in an eight-man game is between a ten and a jack.)

As far as analysis is concerned, there should be few problems. If you give your opponent a good hole card (which is generally right to do), his entire hand is known. Thus most decisions can be made on a purely mathematical basis. Table 7.8 is about all that one needs to make expert plays. It is useful to note from the table that tens and jacks do not necessarily ruin a hand. Entries 1 and 2 are good examples of this.

TABLE 7.8
Chances of Winning in a Variety of Contests
(Five-Card Stud for Low)

Entry	Hand 1	Hand 2	Hand 3
1	102 44.6%*	74 55.4%	
2	1032 48.4%	754 51.6%	
3	Q32 40.7%	754 59.3%	
4	1032A 40.5%	754A 59.5%	
5	J32A 36.2%	754A 63.8%	
6	Q32A 32.6%	754A 67.4%	
7	K32A 25.5%	754A 74.5%	
8	1032 28.6%	754 38.8%	964 32.6%
9	J32 24.8%	754 41.4%	964 33.8%
10	Q32 20.6%	754 42.5%	964 36.9%
11	1032A 22.3%	754A 45.5%	9642 32.2%
12	J32A 16.1%	754A 49.1%	9642 34.8%
13	Q32A 11.6%	754A 51.5%	9642 36.9%
14	K32A 6.2%	754A 53.1%	9642 40.7%

* Probability of winning in a showdown.

BETTING STRATEGY

Most betting problems occur when you have a vastly superior board but have paired, and you want to determine whether your opponents are going to drop if you bet. For instance, you may hold $\underline{8}2\,3\,8$ and your expert opponent may show $\underline{?}4\,5\,Q$. In a low-limit game it may be right for him to call now, in which case he'd almost certainly call on the next round. Consequently, since you virtually can't win, you'd only be throwing away money by betting. As an illustration, suppose there is $50 in the pot and the limit is $10. In this case your opponent couldn't pay more than $20 to have a showdown, so using Rule 7.1b with $k=\frac{2}{5}$, he would only need a $\frac{\frac{2}{5}}{1+\frac{4}{5}}=22\%$ chance to call. However, even if you had a good low card, entry 6 of Table 7.8 would still give him a 32.6% chance. Therefore he has a clearcut call, so it would be wrong to bet.

CALLING STRATEGY

With few exceptions, a decision to call should be made on the assumption that your opponent has a good hole card. True, he could be a bluffer who plays with anything, but this should become apparent in short order. Most players play relatively tight (it's not hard to get two cards under a nine) and they often fold when they pair up. It is useful, however, to remember that a player who bets is much more likely to be paired than one who calls. For example, suppose player A shows $\underline{?}2\,3\,4$ and player B shows $\underline{?}A\,10\,5$. Player A might find it to his advantage to bet even though paired. Player B, on the other hand, would almost certainly drop with a pair. Thus we see that if player A now catches a king and player B catches a six, player A must count on player B holding a pair of sixes to win. This probability is too small to generally warrant a call. However, if player A catches the six and player B the king, then player B may actually have a good chance. Even if player A's first four cards were unpaired, the last card will pair him about 1 time in 6. If any one of the three, four, or six could pair player A, his chances of being paired would be about 1 in 3. Consequently, player B should almost always call if his pot odds are over 5 to 1, and he may have a call against some players even if his pot odds are only 2 to 1.

In intermediate rounds the probability of an active player holding a pair is especially small, because there are only one or two cards that can pair him. Therefore it is generally correct to assume that active players are not paired. The following two problems illustrate how calling decisions may be handled. The problems require the use of Table 7.8 and either Rule 7.1a or 7.1b. You should assume that the active players have good hole cards.

PROBLEM

In pot limit you hold $\underline{4}62J$ and your opponent shows $\underline{?}A57$. There is $40 in the pot. He bets $40. What do you do?

Answer: In this case the cost of a showdown will effectively be $40, since the player who makes the best board will claim by betting the pot. Using Rule 7.1b with $k = 1$, you need a $\frac{1}{1+2} = 33\%$ chance to call. Entry 5 of Table 7.8 gives you about a 36% chance, assuming that you actually get to have a showdown. This figure overestimates your actual chances by about 3%, because you won't get to see your opponent's hand when he pairs his hole card.* Therefore your actual chances are about 33%, so your correct play is a toss-up.

PROBLEM

You hold $\underline{A}2310$ against two players who show $\underline{?}457$ and $\underline{?}269$. There is $55 in the pot. The limit for the next two rounds is $20. The $\underline{?}457$ bets $20, and your other opponent calls. What do you do?

---

* He won't get to see your hand at times when you pair up also, but this only makes a difference when he catches an ace, a king, or a queen.

Answer: Entry 11 of Table 7.8 gives you about a 22% chance of winning, assuming that neither opponent has a bad hole card. Using Rule 7.1a with $x = .22$, the cost of a showdown should not exceed $\dfrac{.22}{1 - .66} \times \$55 \approx \$35$. In this case you may have to call on the last round because you'll be getting 7 to 1 odds, but you won't always have to call. The cost of a showdown should not exceed \$30 on the average. Therefore you should call.

8

HIGH-LOW

In High-Low, as the name implies, the highest and lowest hands split the pot. I will assume that straights and flushes can be counted for low as well as for high, and that an ace may be counted as either high or low (or both). Consequently, 5 4 3 2 A is the best possible low, and a player holding A A 2 4 6 8* has a pair of aces for high and 8 6 4 2 A for low.

My discussion of High-Low Seven-Card Stud assumes an intermediate limit,** but much of the analysis will be accurate for all limits. I will always assume a full game with eight players. If your game is shorthanded, reduce the requirements I give.

DECLARATION

There are three different ways of conducting the showdown at High-Low. In one method, called *cards speak* (short for cards speak for themselves), the players simply lay

---

* Whenever the suits of cards are not mentioned, you should assume that they are irrelevant.

** By an "intermediate limit" I mean a limit that is roughly one or two times the size of the total ante.

down their hands and the highest and lowest hands split the pot. In the other methods there is a "declaration." Each player must declare whether he is trying for high, for low, or for both high and low. If he declares "high," he must beat all the other players who have declared high, and he is not eligible to win for low. If he declares high-low (swings), he must win both ways.

The methods using a declaration differ as to whether the declaration is simultaneous or consecutive. In games with a *simultaneous declaration*, the players begin by secretly placing chips or some other tokens in their closed fists. (This is usually done with both hands under the table.) The number of chips a player puts in his hand determines his direction. For example, zero chips might be low; one chip, high; and two chips, high-low. Once each player has put zero, one, or two chips in his hand, the players then bring their hands up from under the table and simultaneously expose their chips. (This is the point at which they simultaneously declare.) If one direction remains undeclared, the entire pot is awarded to the winner of the other direction.

When a *consecutive declaration* is used, the last bettor or raiser must orally declare first. The other active players then declare behind him in clockwise order. If there was no bet or raise on the last round, the high board declares first.

I will assume throughout this chapter that showdowns are performed using a simultaneous declaration, since this is rapidly becoming the most popular method. There are, however, a few points about the other methods worth mentioning.

Cards Speak

In cards speak, virtually all initial play should be for low. A high hand like three kings will almost never win more than half the pot, and it may well win less. Consider for example a

Seven-Card Stud game with a $3 limit and a total ante of $1. Player A, showing ??3, opens for $1; two others call; and we call, holding 5̲ 5̲ 5. On the next round player A bets the limit, the others drop, and we call. Player A continues to bet the limit and we call. At the end there will be $29 in the pot, and we will have put in $13, with virtually no chance for low. When we win high, we get back $14.50 for a gain of $1.50. When we lose, we lose $13. Thus we see that three of a kind is almost a death trap in cards speak. It seldom wins for low and it need not win high. When it does win, it wins almost nothing.

Because a player can win for either high or low without declaring, it is particularly important to watch for situations in which you must have a winner in at least one direction. For example, suppose you hold 8̲5̲4810106̲ and your opponent shows ??66AQ? in different suits. If he can beat a ten for low he can only have a pair of sixes for high. Hence you have a guaranteed winner in at least one direction, and you can safely bet the limit.

Consecutive Declaration

In consecutive declaration the primary objective should be to declare last, since this is generally an advantage with both good and bad hands. Not infrequently, everyone will check on the final round and the high board will have to declare first. Because of this very real possibility, the player with the high board is usually at a considerable disadvantage. Consequently, hands like 2̲5̲77 are really quite weak.

If you are to the left of the high board, you will often gain by driving that hand out so as to improve your position. For example, suppose the game is Seven-Card Stud; player A shows ??233K, you have 7̲2̲492Q, and B shows ??AK67. Player A is to your right, B to your left. You would do very well with A gone, since then you could declare last and win at least half the pot. With A in the contest, however, your prospects are not so rosy, since you cannot escape if A and B go in opposite directions.

HIGH-LOW SEVEN-CARD STUD

PLAYING REQUIREMENTS

The accepted rule in this game is to start off by playing for low. If you start off with K̲K̲3, you are destined for a high declare, but you may find a number of initially low hands ending up making trips or aces up and beating you for high. Consequently, to allow for the possibility of making either a high or a low hand, it is best to start out by playing for low. There are exceptions, however. A low three of a kind is an excellent starting hand because it will generally win for high without improvement, and may even win the whole pot. A pair of aces with a low card is also an excellent hand. A concealed low pair with a low kicker is not really a good hand, but it should be played for the purposes of variation. If you always play with three low cards, your hands will be extremely easy to read and you will lose the element of deception which is so vital in High-Low. The following hands should probably be played in most games:

1. Any three low cards to a seven
2. Three cards to a flush with a low upcard and at most one high hole card
3. Any three of a kind
4. A pair of aces and a low card
5. Any low pair with an ace in the hole

Optional:

6. Three to an eight with an ace and a five or lower
7. Three to an eight with a concealed two flush
8. An 876
9. A concealed pair below nines with a low upcard
10. Three cards to a flush with two high hole cards (eight or over) and a low upcard

The optional hands are clearly inferior, but they should generally be played for the purposes of variation. In a loose game it may be necessary to occasionally play hands like 7̲5̲K of spades, A̲KK, or even A̲7J in different suits. The best time to play such hands is when most players have bad upcards.

STAYING AFTER THE SECOND CARD

A decision to stay after the second card should at least partially depend on what the other players are showing. When most hands look low, flush draws and high trips should do well, but a hand like 2̲5̲72 may not. However, 2̲5̲72 will do well when most hands look high. In general, you should not play an obviously high hand against a single opponent.

List ed below are most of the problem hands that appear after the second upcard. Hands in the first category should generally be played for at least one more round. Hands in the second category should be dropped if a large number of low cards appear. Hands in the third category should almost always be dropped.

Possible Problem Hands After the Second Upcard

Fair Hands

1. 2̲2̲37, 7̲2̲32, 7̲3̲22
2. A̲A̲3K
3. ♥K♥3̲♥2♥Q
4. 5̲4̲3K

Questionable Hands	5. 7̲3̲2 10, 7̲3̲2 K
	6. 8̲7̲6 K
Bad Hands	7. ♥K̲ ♥Q̲ ♥3♣2, ♥K̲ ♥3̲ ♥2 ♣Q̲
	8. 2̲2̲3 K

READING HANDS

Since High-Low combines a little of high Stud with a little of low, techniques for reading hands in the Stud chapter may be applied with some success to High-Low. In particular, Table 7.7 should be quite useful. That table gives the probability that a tight player will make a hand when he catches a number of low upcards.

Also useful is a knowledge of the distribution of playable hands. This information is contained in Tables 8.1a and 8.1b. Notice that most playable hands consist of three low cards. Therefore you can always assume that a conservative player has two low cards in the hole until his actions indicate that some other hand is more likely.

TABLE 8.1a
Probabilities of Various Initial Hands Given an Upcard of a Seven or Below

Hand	Approximate Probability
1. Any three low cards to a seven	19%
2. Three cards to a flush, with at least two cards seven or lower	4%
3. Three of a kind	$\frac{1}{4}$%
4. A pair of aces and a low card	
An ace is the upcard	1%
An ace is not the upcard	$\frac{1}{2}$%
5. Three to an eight, with an ace and a five or lower	
An ace is the upcard	5%
The upcard is a 5, 4, 3, or 2	1%

TABLE 8.1a (Continued)

Hand	Approximate Probability
6. Three to an eight, with a concealed two flush	1½%
7. An 876	1%
8. A concealed pair below nines	3%
9. Three cards to a flush, with two high cards	1%
10. Any low pair, with an ace in the hole (the upcard is not an ace)	1%
Total when the upcard is a 5, 4, 3, or 2	31¼%

TABLE 8.1b
Distribution of Hands in Table 8.1a

Hand	Fraction of All Hands
Three low cards to an eight or better	71%
A pair	15%
Three flush with two low cards	10%
Three flush with two high cards	3%
Three of a kind	1%

Reading Hands in Games with an Optional Buy (Replacement)

In games with a replacement, a player has the option of replacing a card he doesn't want. For example, if you were playing Six-Card Stud with a replace, you would have the *option* of receiving another card either faceup or facedown, depending on whether the card you threw away was faceup or facedown. In such games the card your opponent throws away and the time he takes to decide may tell you a lot about his hand. For example, suppose your single opponent throws a nine from ??3499 in Six-Card Stud. You hold 867528. If your opponent had another pair with the nines, he probably would have rapped pat or thrown away a low card. Consequently, there is a strong inference that his present hand is something like 62349. You could draw to the straight, but you really don't need more than two eights to win for high. Therefore you should refuse to replace. If he catches an eight or lower, you should go high only. If he catches a bad card or a low pair, you should swing.

EXERCISES IN READING HANDS*

Problem: A mediocre but conservative opponent shows ??32KQ?, and you hold 8363872. How do you declare?

Answer: Because your board is so strong, your opponent probably won't go low with worse than an eight. Therefore you won't make any money by going low. Your chances of winning for high are actually quite good, because your opponent's most likely first six cards are something like 7532KQ (Table 8.1a or 8.1b). Therefore you should go high.

Problem: Player A shows ??384 and B shows ??4QJ. The 4, Q, and J are all spades. You hold A74A8. Player A bets and B calls. Both players are conservative. There are 4 bets in the pot. What do you do?

Answer: Player A is favored to already have an eight since he was probably drawing to 7xx or better, and the four is unlikely to have paired him. B is likely to have a flush, since few conservative players would call with 634QJ in different suits or with 664QJ. It looks like you're in the middle, so you should drop.

Problem: You are quite pleased to have 67453QK. Your opponents show ??A3JK? and ??784K?. The betting in your small-limit game has been fairly intense, so there is a big pot. You don't know whether to swing or not. You have the low board, so you must speak first. What do you do?

Answer: The main objective should be to determine your opponents' hands rather than to try to win a few extra bets.

---

* Whenever the suits of cards are not mentioned, assume that they are irrelevant.

If you check, an opponent with a good hand may bet or look irritated that you didn't. If you bet you won't be able to see these reactions. Consequently, I favor a check.

*MATHEMATICAL CONSIDERATIONS**

As was the case in low-limit Stud, the High-Low player frequently finds himself at a critical point in play where he has to decide either to get out or to stay on till the showdown. In these situations the requirements for staying should be considerably tighter than they were in one-winner games. This is because the pot is split, so a player's pot odds will typically be somewhat less than half of what they would be ordinarily. As an example, consider a contest with three players, A, B, and C. Player A has a low lock; B and C are competing for high. It is the final round. Player A bets the pot, and B calls. In this case C will be risking 1 bet to win 1 bet: His pot odds will be 1 to 1. In the same situation in a one-winner game, his pot odds would be 3 to 1. Thus he needs a significantly better chance to call in High-Low.

The following two rules should be helpful for resolving calling problems in low-limit games. They are the counterparts of Rules 7.1a and 7.1b.

RULE 8.1a: Suppose that after you call and others call, there will be n players in the pot. If a showdown will cost k times what was in the pot at the beginning of the round, then you should call only if your probability of not losing is at least $\dfrac{2k}{nk+1}$.

EXAMPLE OF USE: —————————————————————————

You and a single opponent are in the pot. You have an obvious set of three kings and are worried that he may make a straight, which could beat you for high. If there is $1 in the

* This section is fairly difficult and can be skipped.

pot and it will cost \$10 to declare, then your chances of winning for high should be at least $\frac{2 \times 10}{(2 \times 10) + 1} \approx 95\%$ to warrant a call. In other words, it will often be better to drop.

The next rule tells you the maximum you should pay to reach a showdown when you know what your chances are.

RULE 8.1b: Suppose that after you call and others call, there will be n players in the pot. If your probability of winning at least half the pot is x, then you should call whenever x is at least $2/n$. If x is less than $2/n$, then you should call if the cost of a showdown will not exceed $\frac{x}{2 - nx}$ times what was in the pot at the beginning of the round.

EXAMPLE OF USE

You hold $\underline{3}748$ while your opponents show ??KK and ??34. At the beginning of this round there was \$2 in the pot. The player with ??34 bets the limit of \$1 and your other opponent raises. Since your opponent with the low board may be paired, you estimate your chances for low at about 50%. What do you do?

Answer: You have virtually no chance for high, so your chances of winning in total are about 50%. Plugging $x = .50$ and $n = 3$ into Rule 8.1b, we see that you should call if the cost of reaching a showdown will not exceed $\frac{.50}{2 - 3(.50)} \times \$2 = \$2$. This contest figures to cost substantially more than \$2, so you should fold.

The important point to observe about the preceding problem is that you need more than a 50% chance to call. This is because the pot is split: For every dollar you put in, you get back only half a dollar profit when you win. Consequently, you need to be almost a 2 to 1 favorite in order to call.

REPRESENTATION

While it is important to read opponents' hands, it is equally important to bet in such a way that opponents will misread your hand. In other words, you should attempt to "represent" a hand that you do not have.

Consider the following situation: You hold 7̲4̲A22; your opponents show ?̲?̲538 and ?̲?̲736. If one of them bets, your best play is probably to raise. This way, you are playing the hand *as though* you had three deuces or aces up. If the going gets rough, your raise may pave the way for an unopposed high declaration later on. Since your chances of winning for low are almost the same as anyone else's, the raise probably won't cost anything. If you do make a good low hand you will have a much better chance of winning the whole pot.

Another example of a representation would be a bet into a possible swing hand to discourage a high-low call. This bet should be made only if your hand gives the impression that you could conceivably win in either direction. For example, you might hold 8̲2̲♣5♣3♣4♥5Q̲, and another player might show ?̲?̲6453?̲. A bet on your part may persuade him to declare only one way. This would give you a 50% chance of winning half the pot.

PROBLEM ───────────────────────────────────────

In Six-Card Stud with a replace, you hold 6̲2̲3A88 and your opponent shows ?̲?̲3499. He throws away the four. It's your turn to replace. What do you do?

Answer: Rap pat. This play may scare your opponent into going low since you would make the same play with aces up

or with three eights. Any other play either gives you a
chance to lose or leaves you with almost no chance of winning more than half the pot.

HIGH-LOW DRAW

High-Low Draw is played just like Draw or Lowball, except
that the high and low hands split the pot. It is best played
with a simultaneous form of declaration, and I will assume
that it is being played in this fashion. Because of the declaration, there are three rounds of betting: a round before the
draw, a round after the draw, and a round after the declare.
To fix the discussion, I will assume that the limit equals the
total ante on all three rounds. If your game has a somewhat
larger total ante, reduce the requirements I give.

Your play in High-Low Draw should be almost exclusively
with either pat hands or one-card draws. A two-card draw
to a low hand is too weak to play. A two-card draw to a high
hand is acceptable, but if you only draw two cards to high
hands, your opponents will have an easy low declare whenever you draw two. As a result, it is best not to draw two
cards at all. True, it may be slightly harder to improve, but
the cost of giving your opponents an easy way out will be
much more substantial.

There is a similar disadvantage in betting, calling, or raising with primarily high (or low) hands, and we can state the
following general rule.

RULE 8.2: Against good players, one should bet, call, and
raise with approximately as many high hands as low ones.
Also, one should declare high approximately as often as low
with pat hands and one-card draws.

Rule 8.2 has the following simple consequence: you should play roughly as many high hands pat as you play low ones pat.

A number of poker books have asserted that most hands played pat will be low. If your opponents read those books, most of your pat hands should be high! The logic behind this last statement is best seen by an example. Suppose that you open and one player calls, after which you rap pat. If your opponent infers that you are more likely to have a low hand, then he will go high unless he makes a good low. This means that you will be more likely to win the whole pot when your hand is high. From this it follows that more pat highs will be worth playing than pat lows.

The need to declare low as often as high with one-card draws arises primarily when you are up against another one-card draw. For example, if you declared low two thirds of the time in these situations, your opponent would always go high unless he made a reasonable low, in which case he would come after you. This would help him and hurt you.

OPENING REQUIREMENTS

Opening requirements should vary with position, but jacks up, a 96543, and a one-card draw to a six will always be profitable to open. Hands like 7654 and 7543 are also acceptable. If you want to make sure that you open with as many high pat hands as low ones, rap pat with queens up, aces up, and with all even three of a kinds (deuces, fours, sixes, etc.).*

The hands I have mentioned will always be profitable to open, but it may be better to sandbag. You will have to decide this for yourself. The extent to which players sandbag will affect the profitability of opening with mediocre hands in a good position. A pair of kings or an 8763 should be

---

* An alternate approach would be to rap pat with three deuces or better. However, if you did this you would be marked with less than three of a kind whenever you drew one.

profitable to open with when you are last to speak — if sand-bagging is not rampant. Of course, if you open with kings and encounter competition, it may be best to draw one.

CALLING STRATEGY

A good player should not be called with less than a 1 in 4 chance of beating him when you go in his direction. This is the absolute minimum, and you are advised not to call in a mediocre position* with less than a 1 in 3 chance. Since draws to rough four flushes and high four straights have less than a 1 in 5 chance of materializing, they should generally be dropped. The same goes for all high hands that can't beat the worst high hand your opponent opens with. A pair of aces may represent a call against a player who opened in a good position. If you do decide to call, draw one unless he raps pat.

The figure of 1 in 4 assumes that your opponent plays as many high hands as low ones. If, for example, you know that he plays more low hands, then you can afford to call with somewhat weaker one-card draws. When you miss, you can escape easier; and when you catch, you are more likely to find him going the same direction.

RAISING STRATEGY

Raising requirements should depend on the position of the opener. A hand that looks as good as 3456 does not warrant a raise against someone who opened in a bad position. True, the hand may become a swing hand, but it is basically only slightly better than a one-card draw.

A good rule of thumb is that a raising hand should be able to beat the opener at least 60% of the time when you go the same direction. Against a player who follows the standards

---

* The best position in this case is just to the opener's right.

of jacks up, etc., which I set earlier, this means that you need at least three sevens or an 8 6 4 3 2 to raise.

When you open and get raised, you should generally call since the raiser will often be going in the other direction. If he's your only opponent and you have a pat low, your correct play will often be to break. It won't make any difference whether you break or not when he's going high. When he's going low, you may as well try to win.

Always raise with a one way lock. If you flat call to sucker people in, one of them will probably walk off with half the pot.

BETTING AFTER THE DRAW

In the betting round immediately following the draw, it is particularly important to bet with approximately as many low hands as high ones. If you bet with mostly low hands, your opponents will have an easy high declare whenever you bet.

Suppose now that you opened on the first round and that one player called and drew one. In this case there will be three bets in the pot. If you bet after the draw, he should call regardless of his hand since he stands to gain half of 3 bets, or $1\frac{1}{2}$ bets, if he guesses right. Since he should always call, you can afford to bet a hand that figures to win slightly over 60% of the time when you both go the same direction, i.e., a good nine. If you bet in this fashion, he can bet a ten or a jack when you draw one and check. However, he should not bet a ten if you rap pat and then check, since you would not rap pat with a jack.

After the declare you won't be called as often, but you can still bet a good nine if your opponent merely called your bet on the second round. You can bet a ten if you checked on the second round and he checked also.

In three-player contests, the requirements for betting after the draw should be tightened to the point where the first player to speak needs a good seven to bet against two one-card draws.

PROBLEMS

Problem: You open in a good position with A A K 9 2 and get raised by a player who figures to play his hand pat. You decide to call, although you're sure he's not bluffing. How many cards do you take?

Answer: There is no point in being deceptive here. Your draw will not affect your opponent's declare. Therefore, if you intend to go high, draw three.

Problem: You open in a good position with 8 7 5 2 and get called by one player, who draws one card. Most of his one-card draws are to low hands. You make a pair of fives and check. He bets and you call. How do you declare?

Answer: Go high. The chances are too great that he has a better low hand.

Problem: Take the previous problem, except that your opponent raised and then drew one. Now what?

Answer: A raise with a one-card draw to a low hand is a poor play since the hand has no chance of making a high and needs to be lucky to make a low. Such a play may not be beyond your present opponent, but on the average he is more likely to have a high hand. Consequently I favor a low declare.

9

RULES FOR
GENERAL PLAY

This chapter is meant for the advanced player who wants additional insight into poker in general. Those of you who are mathematically inclined should also read the Appendix, which presents examples of how some of the more complicated strategies were derived. While the discussion here will have general applicability, it is more applicable to Draw and Lowball, and it is probably best to think of one of those games as you read.

The amount of mathematics you need to understand this chapter is minimal. However, you should understand the difference between probabilities and odds. When the odds against something occurring are 3 to 1, the probability of its occurring is $\frac{1}{4}$. More generally, when the odds against something occurring are P to 1, the probability of its occurring is $\frac{1}{P+1}$. I will frequently use the terminology "of the time" when I refer to probabilities. For example, when I say that someone should drop one third of the time, I mean that he should drop 1 time in 3. A flat limit will be assumed throughout the chapter.

RULES FOR THE FIRST ROUND

OPENING STRATEGY

There is no simple rule for computing good opening strategies for all games. However, the following *conservative* rule is quite good for high games.

RULE 9.1: If the odds against a hand being high (low) are less than the odds offered by the pot, the hand will be profitable to open.

When we denote the number of bets in the total ante by P, Rule 9.1 is equivalent to saying that it will be profitable to open any hand that has a probability of at least $\frac{1}{P+1}$ of being high (low)

EXAMPLE ————————————————————————

If $P=1$, any hand that has a probability of at least $\frac{1}{1+1}=\frac{1}{2}$ of being high (low) will be profitable to open.

Notice that Rule 9.1 says nothing about the possibilities of sandbagging. It also says nothing about the profitability of opening with weaker hands. It merely says that a certain class of hands will definitely be profitable to open.

The logic behind Rule 9.1 is as follows. In high games it generally doesn't pay for opponents to call if they have inferior hands. (I will assume this to be the case.) Consequently, if they know approximately what your minimum opening hand is, and they can't beat it, they won't call. Therefore, when your minimum opening hand is high, you should win the total ante of P bets. When someone has you beat, you figure to lose at most the bet you put in.* If you can win P bets once for every P times you lose part of a bet, you will come out ahead. Therefore in high games it will

* You can always drop if you get raised. It's true that you may be bluffed occasionally, but the probability of this is small.

pay to open when the odds against your having the best hand are less than P to 1.

In low games the analysis is more complicated, but it often turns out that one should open with a hand that has almost no chance of being low. For example, the odds are 3 to 1 against 8543 being low in an eight-man game. However, it should still be opened when the pot offers odds of slightly over 1 to 1.

Rule 9.1 can be used in conjunction with any "distribution of hands" table like Tables 3.10, 5.10, 7.1, or 7.3. For example, suppose the total ante equals 2 bets in a pass and out Draw game. In this case Rule 9.1 says to open any hand that has a probability of at least $\frac{1}{3}$ of being high. If you are in third position, Table 3.10 says that a pair of eights has a 37% probability (slightly over a probability of $\frac{1}{3}$) of being high. Consequently, you should definitely open with eights or better. The actual minimum opening hand should be sixes (Table 3.1).

CALLING STRATEGY

The following well-known rule is a special case of Rules 7.1a and 7.1b.

RULE 9.2: Call if the odds against your winning are less than the odds offered by the pot.

When the pot contains P bets, Rule 9.2 is equivalent to saying that you should call if your chances of winning are at least $\frac{1}{P+1}$.

EXAMPLE OF USE ——————————————————————

Suppose your Draw game has a total ante of 1 bet, and the opener is marked with at least jacks. You are in zeroth position. In this case your chances of winning are the same as your chances of beating the opener. Since there are 2 bets in the pot, you need at least a $\frac{1}{2+1} = \frac{1}{3}$ chance against him (Rule 9.2). It may be verified that a pair of kings has a 40% chance against someone with jacks or better, whereas a pair of queens has only a 29% chance (Table 3.12). Therefore, kings should be the minimum calling hand in this situation.

EXAMPLE OF USE

Again, your Draw game has a total ante of 1 bet. You open and someone raises. He figures to have kings or better. Since the pot currently contains 4 bets, you need at least a $\frac{1}{4 + 1} = 20\%$ chance to call. With aces, you would have a 37% chance (entry 17, Table 3.12), but with kings you would only have a 19% chance. Therefore, assuming that the raiser doesn't bluff, you need at least aces (fifth row, Table 3.8a).

RAISING STRATEGY AGAINST ONE OPPONENT

The following rules are fairly good for Draw and Low-ball. The rules assume that the raiser has good position. When the raiser has bad position, he may have to tighten his requirements because of the threat from players behind him.

RULE 9.3a (DRAW): If your opponent's worst likely hand is kings or less, raise if you have at least a 50% chance of winning in a showdown. If your opponent's worst likely hand is two pairs, raise if you have at least a 60% chance.

EXAMPLE OF USE

Suppose your single opponent figures to have jacks or better. According to entry 24 of Table 3.12, a pair of aces should have a 53% chance against him. Therefore it represents a borderline raise.

The logic behind Rule 9.3a may be explained by looking at two examples. Let's see first why you only need a 50% chance when your opponent's hand may be weak.

Suppose that you hold aces and your opponent has a smaller pair. In this case he has a 22% chance of winning (entry 1, Table 3.11). If the total ante is one bet and you raise, he will be getting 4 to 1 odds, so he only needs a 1 in 5 (20%) chance to call. This means that he will gain by calling, so you would rather that he drop. The worst that can happen to you, therefore, is that he always calls. If this happens, you will lose slightly by raising if your hand has only a 50% chance of winning in a showdown, because he will occasionally reraise. In practice, however, he won't always call, so the figure of 50% is about right.

Now suppose that you have jacks up and your opponent has a smaller two pairs. Most raising situations in which both players have strong hands are reraising situations, and I will assume this to be the case. If you open, he raises, and you reraise, he will be getting 6 to 1 odds, so he needs at least a 1 in 7 or 14% chance to call. However, in this case he only has a 9% chance (entry 5, Table 3.11). This means that he will do better by *dropping*, so you would rather that he call. Now the worst that can happen is that he always drops when you have him beat.

He should drop about one third* of the time, and if he does so, you will need more than a 50% chance in order to raise.**_ It turns out that you need approximately a 60% chance.

Rule 9.3b (LowBall): Make an initial raise if you have at least a 48% chance of winning in a showdown. Reraise if you have at least a 75% chance of being low *before the draw*.

---

* By reraising you risk 2 additional bets to win 4. Your opponent must therefore call at least two thirds of the time to keep you honest (Rule 9.4).

** If he always called, you would need slightly over a 50% chance. You do better when he calls with an inferior hand than you do when he drops with an inferior hand. Therefore, if he frequently drops with inferior hands, you will need more than a 50% chance.

EXAMPLE OF USE ———————————————————————

You open and your opponent raises. He figures to have 9864A or better. Since 9864A is hand number 105 in Table 5.8, you need at least hand number 105/4 ≈ 26, or 85432, to reraise.*

The logic behind Rule 9.3b is similar to that for Rule 9.3a. The worst that can happen when you raise with a borderline hand in Lowball is that your opponent always calls, in which case you would need slightly over a 50% chance of winning in a showdown to make raising profitable. However, since your raise will often persuade your opponent to break a superior hand, the figure of 50% can actually be shaded down a bit.

When you are considering reraising, you need a particularly good hand because your raise will often persuade your opponent to break and hence give him a chance of winning where before he had none.

RULES FOR THE FINAL ROUND

In Chapters 4 and 6 two different types of strategies were presented. It will be convenient here to refer to those strategies as best informed strategies and best uninformed strategies. P will stand for the number of bets that are in the pot after someone has bet. In other words, to the caller there will be P bets in the pot, whereas to the bettor there

---

*This hand is only an approximation to the correct strategy, since Rule 9.3b is only an approximate rule. The correct minimum reraising hand is 8542A (Table 5.4).

were only $P - 1$. Most rules in this section have already been discussed in Chapters 4 and 6.

BEST INFORMED CALLING STRATEGY

The best informed calling strategy after the draw is given by Rule 9.2. Suppose your single opponent bets, after which there are P bets in the pot. If he bluffs more than once for every P times he bets legitimately, you should call with any hand that can beat a bluff (Rule 9.2). If he bluffs less than once for every P times he bets legitimately, you should drop unless you can beat some of his legitimate hands (also Rule 9.2). If he bluffs exactly once for every P times he bets legitimately, it won't matter what you do with your problem hands. It is perhaps not surprising, then, that his best uninformed strategy is to bluff exactly once for every P times that he bets legitimately. This will be discussed more in the bluffing section.

BEST UNINFORMED CALLING STRATEGY AGAINST ONE OPPONENT

We have already discussed this strategy in some detail in Chapter 4. Let's agree to call the first player to speak player 1, and his opponent player 2. With few exceptions, player 2 should drop in such a fashion that player 1 breaks even, on the average, by bluffing.*

We can get a feel for what this means by looking at an example. Suppose the game is Draw poker, with an Ante and Straddle. The player in seventh position opens with aces, and the Straddle calls with a medium pair. After the draw there are $P - 1$ bets in the pot. If the Straddle fails to

---

* In a three-player contest with players 1, 2, and 3, a similar statement can be made. Players 2 and 3 should both drop *together* in such a fashion that player 1 breaks even, on the average, by bluffing. Rule 9.4 can also be stated for three-player contests.

improve, the opener will gain nothing by "bluffing" with aces. He only gains by bluffing with aces if the Straddle improves and then drops. To insure that the opener breaks even by bluffing, the Straddle should call or raise with $P-1$ improved hands for each improved hand that he drops. Equivalently, he should drop 1 time out of P when he improves.

This example lays the basis for the following good approximate rule.

RULE 9.4: The second player to speak should drop with all hopeless hands and with 1/P of the hands that can beat a bluff. The hands he drops with should be his worst.

EXAMPLE OF USE (LOWBALL)

Player 1 draws a card and player 2 raps pat. There are 3 final-round bets in the pot. In this situation player 2 would have played as he did with 98765 or better. What is the best hand he should drop with?

Answer: All of player 2's hands can beat a bluff. Therefore, according to Rule 9.4 he should drop with the worst quarter of his hands. Since 98765 is hand number 126 in Table 5.8, the worst hand he should drop with is hand number $\frac{3}{4} \times 126 \approx 95$, this is 98432.

Rule 9.4 works fairly well for both players in Draw, but it tends to overestimate the number of hands that player 1 should call with in Lowball. The reasoning behind this is fairly complicated and is based on the following two observations.

1. Player 2 bets legitimately with more hands than player 1.
2. Player 2 can check with a bad hand such as threes and still win the pot, whereas player 1 cannot. If player 1 checks and player 2 has a worse hand, he will bluff

player 1 out. The consequence is that player 2 gains less by bluffing with bad hands.

When player 1 calls somewhat less than Rule 9.4 indicates, he allows player 2 to make some money by bluffing, but he reduces the amount of money that player 2 makes by betting legitimately. Since player 2 bets quite often and cannot gain much by bluffing (observations 1 and 2), such a strategy turns out to be beneficial for player 1. Player 2, however, does better by following Rule 9.4.

BEST UNINFORMED STRATEGY FOR CALLING AFTER A RAISE

This strategy is based on the same principles as the strategy for calling after a bet. The difference is that your opponent risks twice as much to bluff by raising. Consequently, you can afford to drop twice as often. The following rule gives the best strategy:

RULE 9.5: If the pot currently contains R bets, drop $2/R$ of the time.* Drop with your worst hands.

BEST INFORMED BLUFFING STRATEGY

This strategy was at least partially covered in the calling section. Let's assume that the pot contains $P - 1$ bets. In a two-player contest, the first player to speak gains by bluffing with a hopeless hand if his opponent drops over $1/P$ of the time. The second player gains only if the first player drops over $1/P$ of the time *with a better hand.* In larger contests, a player will generally gain only if his opponents all drop together over $1/P$ of the time. Essentially this means that a

---

* R is used here because P stands for the number of bets that are in the pot after someone has bet. R will always be greater than 3 since I am assuming a flat limit.

player should bluff more if his opponents call less than they should. He should never bluff if they call too frequently.

BEST UNINFORMED BLUFFING STRATEGY

As mentioned earlier, if the pot will contain P bets after you have bet, an expert will be able to take advantage of you if you bluff either more or less than once for every P times that you bet legitimately. If you bluff too much, he will call excessively and almost all of your bluffs will lose. If you bluff too little, he will rarely call and you will lose money when you bet legitimately. The best uninformed strategy is given by the following rule.

RULE 9.6: If the pot will contain P bets after you have bet, bluff once for every P times that you bet legitimately. Make sure that you bluff with your worst hands.

The reason you should bluff with your worst hands is that it may be more profitable to check with better ones. The best hands to bluff with are those that cannot win if checked.

EXAMPLE OF USE ───────────────────────────

Suppose you make an obvious one-card draw to a straight or flush and fail to improve. There are 6 bets in the pot. Approximately how often should you bet as a bluff in this situation?

Answer: You figure to make a hand about 1 time in 6,* in which case you would bet. If the same situation were repeated 42 times, you would make about 7 legitimate bets, so you should also make 1 illegitimate bet. Hence in the 35 times out of 42 that you don't make a hand, you should bluff once.

EXAMPLE OF USE ───────────────────────────

After drawing one card in Lowball, you routinely bet with 87654 or better whenever the pot contains 4 bets. What hands should you bluff with?

───
* This figure is a slight approximation which combines the possibilities that you may be drawing to either a straight or a flush.

Answer: Rule 9.6 says that you should bluff 1 time for every 5 times that you bet legitimately. You figure to make an eight or better 33% of the time (Table 5.12). Therefore you should bluff with the worst $\dfrac{33\%}{5} = 6.6\%$ of your hands. Using Tables 5.9 and 5.12, this means that you should bluff with 66543 or worse (fourth row, Table 6.2).

The best uninformed raise-bluffing strategy is also given by Rule 9.6. If the pot will contain R bets after you raise, bluff once for every R times that you raise legitimately.

BETTING STRATEGY

The correct time to bet is when a bet figures to be more profitable than a check. Unfortunately, this is often quite hard to determine. A good substitute rule is to bet whenever it is profitable to do so. Since you only gain by betting when your opponent calls and loses, it follows that a bettable hand should win at least half of the time when it is called. Because of the raise danger, a slight safety factor is desirable, and we can state the following good approximate rule:

RULE 9.7: Bet a hand that figures to lose less than two fifths of the time when it is called or raised.

EXAMPLE OF USE ————————————————————

You draw three cards to kings in high Draw and make kings up. A single expert opponent drew three cards also, presumably to aces. There are 3 bets in the pot. Will it be profitable to bet?

Answer: Your opponent is going to have to call (or raise) you about three fourths of the time (Rule 9.4), because all of his hands (including aces) are susceptible to a bluff. He only figures to improve and hence beat you 29% of the time (Table 4.1). According to Rule 9.7, this figure should be less than $\frac{2}{5} \times 75\% = 30\%$. Therefore it will be slightly profitable to bet.

RAISING STRATEGY AGAINST ONE OPPONENT

The idea behind raising is somewhat the same as betting. A raising hand should lose less than half of the time when it is called or raised. If the pot will contain R bets after your raise, you should be called or raised $(R - 2)/R$ of the time (Rule 9.5). Therefore we can state the following rule:

RULE 9.8: If the pot currently contains $R - 2$ bets, raise with a hand that figures to lose less than $.45\left(\dfrac{R-2}{R}\right)$ of the time.

EXAMPLE OF USE ——————————————————————————

Suppose you're playing in a shorthanded Five-Card Stud game and hold $\underline{2}2QJ2$ while your single opponent shows $\underline{?}575K$. Your opponent, a good player, bets the limit. Including his bet, there are now 3 bets in the pot. You know he isn't bluffing. What do you do?

Answer: You can neglect the possibility of a good player having started with $\underline{7}5$. Therefore he must have either three fives or kings up.* There are two fives and three kings, or five possible cards that he could have. Two of the five cards lose for you, so you should expect to lose 40% of the time. According to Rule 9.8 this figure should be less than $.45 \times \frac{3}{5} = 27\%$. Therefore don't raise.

---

* I am assuming here that your opponent's bet tells you nothing about his hand. Some players will not bet with kings up in this situation because they don't feel that it's good enough. Consequently, when they do bet, you can infer that they have three fives. Other players prefer to check with three fives so that they can raise later. When these players bet, you can infer that they have kings up.

APPENDIX

SECTION 1: COMPUTATION OF OPENING STRATEGIES FOR DRAW POKER

It will be shown here that kings should be opened in seventh position when the total ante equals 1 bet.* A similar demonstration will be made for a four flush when the total ante equals 2 bets. These demonstrations should give you a good idea of how opening strategies may be computed in general. It is useful to note that the computations depend on a knowledge of the correct calling and raising strategies. These must be computed beforehand.

Analysis for Kings When the Total Ante Is One Bet

After someone opens, three things can happen. He can be called by one or more players, he can be raised, or he can win the antes without a contest. If the opener's worst likely hand is kings, his opponents should not call with less than aces, and in a bad position they shouldn't call with less than a medium two pairs (Table 3.5a). Their average minimum playing hand should be approximately threes and deuces.

* It is assumed that the game has an equal ante from each player.

197

The probability of any one of seven players getting at least such a hand is the same as the probability that aces will not be high against seven players. Using Table 3.10 (row AA, column 7), this probability is $1 - .56 = .44$. Hence the opener figures to get called or raised roughly 44% of the time. His opponents' average minimum raising hand should be approximately nines up (Table 3.6a). Using Table 3.10 (row 9988, column 7), he should therefore be raised about $1 - .65 = 35\%$ of the time.

When the opener does encounter competition, he will do better when there are many players in the pot. For example, comparing entries 1 and 16 of Table 3.11, we see that his chances go down by only 2% when another player enters the pot. However, his pot odds go up from 2 to 1, to 3 to 1. Consequently, we can underestimate the opener's gain by assuming that he will be raised by one opponent 35% of the time, that he will be called by one opponent 9% of the time, and that he will steal the antes 56% of the time. When he is called by one player, his chances using entries 1 and 2 of Table 3.11 will be about 24%. When he is raised, his chances using entry 4 of Table 3.12 will be around 16%. Let's assume that he calls if raised, although this is not necessarily his best play. His average gain will then be

$$
\begin{array}{lll}
.56(1) & = .56 & \text{(No one calls)} \\
+.09[3(.24) - 1] & \approx -.03 & \text{(One player calls)} \\
+.35[5(.16) - 2] & \approx \underline{-.42} & \text{(One player raises)} \\
& +.11 \text{ of a bet*} &
\end{array}
$$

Hence we see that the opener figures to make slightly over .11 of a bet by opening with kings in seventh seat. If his opponents play poorly he may make less, but he may also make more.

Analysis for Four Flush When the Total Ante Is Two Bets

When the opener's minimum hands are queens and four flushes, most of his opponents should require at least kings to call. However, players in zeroth and first positions may

---

* Neglecting gains and losses on the final round, which are negligible in this case.

call with less. The average minimum calling hand should be around queens. Applying Table 3.10 (row JJ, column 7), we see that the opener should win the ante unopposed about 25% of the time. Since his opponent's average minimum raising hand will be threes and deuces, he should be raised about 44% of the time (Table 3.10, row AA, column 7).

We can underestimate the opener's gain by assuming that he will be called or raised by only one player. His chances in these situations will be those of making a flush, or about 19%. His average gain may therefore be expressed as

$$
\begin{array}{lll}
.25(2) & = .50 & \text{(No one calls)} \\
+ .31[4(.19) - 1] & = -.07 & \text{(One player calls)} \\
+ .44[6(.19) - 2] & = \underline{-.38} & \text{(One player raises)} \\
& +.05 \text{ of a bet} &
\end{array}
$$

Thus we see that opening with a four flush should be profitable.

SECTION 2: COMPUTATION OF OPENING STRATEGIES FOR LOWBALL

Strategies for Lowball may be computed in roughly the same fashion as for Draw. The correct calling and raising strategies are computed first, and then this information is used to check whether various hands will be profitable to open. As an example, let's check whether 8543 will be profitable to open with in seventh seat when the total ante equals 1 bet.*

If the opener's minimum hands are 98765 and 8543, his opponents average worst calling and raising hands should be approximately 8642 and 98543 respectively (Tables 5.2 and 5.4). Using Table 5.10, he should therefore win the antes unopposed 26% of the time, and he should be raised approximately 28% of the time.

If we now assume that the opener is called or raised by only one opponent, we will be *overestimating* his gain.**

---

* It is assumed that the game has an equal ante from each player.

** For example, 8543 has only a 24.8% chance against two substantially smoother one-card draws (entry 9 of Table 5.11). In other words, it breaks about even when two players call, whereas it gains when only one calls.

However, let us do so; 8543 will have about a 21% chance when raised by one player (entries 6 and 7 of Table 5.13), and a 44% chance when called (entry 25 of Table 5.11). Its expectation is therefore approximately

$$
\begin{array}{lll}
.26(1) & = .26 & \text{(No one calls)} \\
+ .46[3(.44) - 1] & = .14 & \text{(One player calls)} \\
+ .28[5(.21) - 2] & = \underline{-.25} & \text{(One player raises)} \\
& +.15 \text{ of a bet} &
\end{array}
$$

The .15 figure neglects a slight positional disadvantage after the draw. When this is taken into account, it becomes clear that 8543 is roughly a minimum opening hand.

SECTION 3: COMPUTATION OF CALLING STRATEGIES FOR DRAW POKER

In this section I will show that a pair of kings represents a minimum calling hand from fourth position against a player with jacks or better when the total ante equals 2 bets. This demonstration should indicate how calling strategies may be computed in general.

A pair of kings has about a 40% chance of beating a player with jacks or better (entries 24 and 25 of Table 3.12). Consequently, if we hold kings in fourth position we will gain approximately .40(4) − 1 = .60 of a bet* by calling when everyone behind us drops. Players behind us shouldn't call with less than aces, and they shouldn't raise with less than threes up. Therefore, using Table 3.10, (row KK, column 4, and row AA, column 4), we will be called about 11% of the time and raised about 28% of the time. Let's assume that at most one other player enters the pot. Our chances when someone calls will be about 18%.** When we are

---

* I am neglecting the final round, whose effect is negligible in this case.

** This figure was determined roughly as follows. When we make trip kings or better, we should win about 80% of the time. When we make kings up, we should win approximately 50% of the time. Our probabilities of making these hands are .13 and .16 respectively (Table 4.1). Therefore our overall chances are approximately .13(.80) + .16(.50) ≈ .18.

raised we figure to lose almost one bet, since it won't help us much to call. Our expected gain by calling is therefore approximately

.61(.60)	= .37	(Everyone behind us drops)
+.11[5(.18) − 1]	= −.01	(One opponent calls)
+.28(−1)	= −.28	(One opponent raises)
	+.08 of a bet	

Thus we see that a pair of kings represents a minimum calling hand.

SECTION 4: ANALYSIS OF A TWO-PLAYER LOWBALL CONTEST

In this section I will attempt to justify the strategies that were presented for a contest involving two one-card draws. This is the easiest type of two-player contest to analyze, because both players start with essentially the same hand. Let's agree to call the first player to speak player 1, and his opponent player 2. I will assume that both players are, on the average, drawing about the same. For example, they may both be drawing to anywhere from 8765 on down. It will be convenient to refer to a hand of rank r as one that figures to lose with probability r. Ranks of various hands may be read off from Table 5.12. For example, 87654 has a rank of .33, and 98765 has a rank of .42. When more accuracy is desired, it is possible to use either Tables 6.17a, b, c, d or Table 5.9, but that won't concern us here.

I claim that the strategies given for each player in Figure 1 represent best uninformed strategies. In other words, when the pot contains 1 bet, player 1 should bet a hand of rank .14 or better, call with a hand of rank .49 or better, and bluff with a hand of rank .93 or worse, etc.

What I will do is simply verify that the strategies for both players satisfy the following intuitively reasonable conditions. This is not in itself a proof, but rather, I hope, a compelling argument.

FIGURE A.1
Best Uninformed Strategies for a Two-Player Contest
When the Pot Contains One Bet

Player 1   Player 2

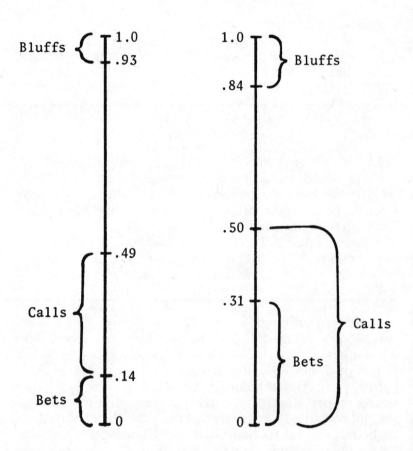

Numbers represent ranks (see text.)

1. Each player's minimum betting hand should be such that it doesn't matter whether the hand is bet or not.
2. Each player must bluff once for every 2 legitimate bets (Rule 9.6).
3. Each player must bluff whenever it is profitable to do so, and must not bluff when it is not profitable to do so.

Verification of Condition 1

If player 1 bets with a hand of rank .14, he will get called and will win $50\% - 14\% = 36\%$ of the time. If he checks he will call and win 31% (player 2 bets) + 16% (player 2 bluffs) − 14% = 33% of the time. Hence, neglecting the raise danger, he makes .03 of a bet more by betting. When the raise possibility is considered, the gains from checking and betting become roughly equal.

Player 2 breaks even by betting a hand of rank .31 since player 1's average calling hand has a rank of $\dfrac{.14 + .49}{2} = .315$.

Verification of Condition 2

Player 1 bets 14% of the time and bluffs 7% of the time. Therefore he bluffs once for every 2 legitimate bets. The same is true for player 2.

Verification of Condition 3

To satisfy condition 3, player 2 should break even by bluffing with his "best" bluffing hand. When he bets with a hand of rank .84, he gains 1 bet whenever player 1 drops with a better hand. This occurs $.84 - .49 = 35\%$ of the time. He loses 1 bet whenever player 1 calls with a better hand, which occurs $.49 - .14 = 35\%$ of the time. Therefore player 2 breaks even by bluffing.

Player 1 can't win by checking with his best bluffing hand since player 2 would bluff him out with an even worse hand. Consequently, player 1 gains by bluffing whenever player

2 drops, which happens 50% of the time. He loses whenever player 2 calls, which also happens 50% of the time. Therefore player 1 breaks even with all his bluffing hands. Condition 3 is satisfied.

GLOSSARY

Acepots: Draw poker in which one needs aces or better to open.

Aces Up: Two pairs, one of which is aces.

Ante: 1. Put chips in the pot before the deal.

      2. In an Ante and Straddle game, the Ante is the player to the left of the dealer. He normally puts in 1 chip before the deal.

Ante and Straddle: A pass and out form of game. Normally, the player to the dealer's left (the Ante) puts in 1 chip, and the player to his left (the Straddle) puts in 2 chips. (The dealer may put in a chip as well.) These 3 (4) chips form the total ante. The chips that each player has contributed are considered part of any bet, call, or raise he may decide to make. So, for example, if the bet is 4 chips, the Ante may call for 3 or raise for 7, and the Straddle may call for 2 or raise for 6.

Blind: In Big Blind games, the Blind is the player who puts in the largest ante.

Bluff: To bet with a losing hand in the hopes of scaring everyone out of the pot.

Board: The upcards in a stud hand.

Boardlock: Same as cinch, lock: a hand that cannot lose.

Break: Draw a card instead of rapping pat.

Bug: In Lowball, a wild card; in high draw, it may be used only as an ace, or in a straight or a flush.

Call: Put in enough chips so that your total contribution equals that of the player who bet or raised just before you.

Cards Speak: A form of High-Low in which there is no declaration.

Check: Put up no chips but reserve the right to call or raise if someone else bets.

Cinch: Same as boardlock, lock: a hand that cannot lose.

Complete Bluff: A first-round bluff made with a hopeless hand.

Consecutive Declaration: A form of High-Low in which the players declare in clockwise order. The last player to bet or raise declares first. If there was no bet or raise on the last round, the high board declares first.

Declaration: An indication, by using tokens or otherwise, that one is going high, low, or high and low. This precedes the final showdown.

Declare: Make a declaration.

Discard: Throw away a card or cards.

Drop: Fold; withdraw from the current deal.

Exposed Pair: Open pair.

Flat Call: Same as call; the "flat" emphasizes that the player did not raise.

Flat Limit: A limit that is constant, say a $2 maximum on each bet or raise.

Flush: Five cards of the same suit.

Fold: Drop.

Four Flush: Four cards of the same suit.

High-Low: A form of poker in which the highest and lowest hands split the pot.

Hole Card: A card dealt facedown in Stud Poker.

Improve: Draw cards that better one's hand.

Inside Straight: A hand like 8754.

Jackpots: A Draw game that requires jacks or better to open.

Kicker: An odd card like an ace or king that is kept when one draws to a small pair or to three of a kind.

Lock: Same as cinch, boardlock: a hand that cannot lose.

Lowball (Misère): A form of Draw Poker in which the lowest hand wins the pot.

Low Poker: A game in which the lowest hand wins the pot.

Open: Make the first bet in the first betting interval.

Open Pair: In Stud Poker, a pair among a player's upcards.

Ordinary Pass and Out: A pass and out game with an equal ante from each player.

Pass: 1. Drop. 2. Check.

Pass and Back In: A game in which checking is allowed on the first round.

Pass and Out: A game in which checking is not allowed on the first round. If no one has opened and it is your turn to speak, you must either bet or drop.

Pat Hand: A hand that is played intact, i.e., a full house.

Percent: A percent sign stands for "over hundred." Thus 55% equals $\frac{55}{100}$, or .55.

Play: 1. Stay in. 2. A creative bluff.

Pot: The chips in the middle of the table.

Pot Limit: The maximum a player can bet or raise is the size of the pot.

Raise: Bet more than is necessary to call.

Rap Pat: Refuse to draw.

Read: Figure out your opponent's hand.

Reraise: To raise a raise.

Rough: Poor.

Round: An interval during which betting is made. In Draw Poker, the first round ends when the draw begins.

Sandbag: To check with the intention of raising later.

Seven-Card Stud: Stud with seven cards. Normally each player receives two cards down and one up at the beginning of the deal. The rest of the cards except the last are dealt faceup.

Sevens Rule: In Lowball (Misère), this rule requires that you bet a seven or better after the draw.

Showdown: The comparison of all hands at the end of the game to determine who wins.

Slowplay: To check or bet a small amount with a good hand.

Smooth: Good.

Snowjob: A pat-hand bluff made with a hand like 4442A in Lowball (Misère).

Stack: The chips belonging to a player.

Stay: Remain in the current deal by calling.

Straddle: 1. The player to the left of the Ante in an Ante and Straddle game. 2. Make a blind raise.

Straight: A hand like 98765.

Suits: Spades, hearts, diamonds, clubs.

Swing: To declare high and low.

Table Stakes: A style of poker in which a player can bet as much as he has on the table at any time.

Total Ante: The total amount anted by all the players.

Two Pairs: A hand containing two pairs with an odd card, e.g., 5522K.

Upcard: A card properly dealt faceup.

Wild Card: A card that may be designated as being anything.

Worst Likely Hand: The worst hand a player is likely to have.